formal aspects of
medieval german poetry

Reinmar the Fiddler. Manesse Manuscript. Fol. 312ro

formal aspects of
medieval german poetry

A   S Y M P O S I U M

Edited with an Introduction by
STANLEY N. WERBOW

PUBLISHED FOR THE DEPARTMENT OF GERMANIC LANGUAGES
OF THE UNIVERSITY OF TEXAS AT AUSTIN BY THE
UNIVERSITY OF TEXAS PRESS, AUSTIN & LONDON

831.109
J76
68494
January 1970

Standard Book Number 292–78420–1
Library of Congress Catalog Card No. 77–82310
Copyright © 1969 by the University of Texas Press
All Rights Reserved
Printed by The University of Texas Printing Division, Austin
Bound by Universal Bookbindery, Inc., San Antonio

contents

formal aspects of
medieval german poetry

introduction

BY STANLEY N. WERBOW

We have learned by now that the intrinsic and main accomplishment of the great *minne* poets was the invention of the forms, the strophic structures and the melody. The development of their art is unfolded in the mastery of ever newer and more magnificent forms and in the most intimate combination of thoughts, of linguistic expression and of strophic forms, that is to say, however, also of the melody.

FRIEDRICH MAURER[1]

The insight expressed by Professor Maurer has in recent decades become almost a commonplace, but academic attention still strays habitually from those "main accomplishments" to the admittedly stereotyped themes and to the content of the poems of the minnesingers. The papers of this symposium were and remain significant in their attention to the formal, the structural, and even the technical aspects of this noteworthy phenomenon of Western European civilization, the courtly love songs of the twelfth and thirteenth centuries and their reflexes even into the fifteenth century.

In our first contribution Professor Taylor surveys for us the boundaries of probability with regard to the music of the minnesongs, leaving open even the possibility that for some medieval minnesong buffs the words were the sole interest. Much as misery loves company, this is small comfort for the loss of what must have been glorious melodies. Who could reconstruct the impact of the halcyon years of Tin Pan Alley from the dumb lyrics of the ten cent song sheets we bought so avidly every week in the thirties?

While Professor Kuhn may appear to be a backslider into content analysis with his elucidation of the social, moral, and personal impli-

[1] "Zur Chronologie der Lieder Heinrichs von Morungen," *Festschrift für Jost Trier zum 70. Geburtstag* (Cologne, 1964), p. 304 (translation mine).

cations of the courtly love convention, he does so with a delicious difference provided by the combination of those main themes with the
form of the singer's very performance.

The development of postclassical *Minnesang* is marked by an in-
crease in ornamentation, notably in the luxuriant use of rhyme. Professor Jackson demonstrates in the work of the fifteenth-century poet-com-
poser Oswald von Wolkenstein how ornamental rhyme and alliteration
may overpower function.

Though musicology has only recently become the focus of considerable attention by Germanists, metrics can be said to have been a prime
object of teaching and research for almost a century. During most of
this time the personalities of the chief practitioners and the development of schools inhibited the reconciliation of opposing views. Professor Heinen calls for an inventory of accepted principles and suggests
means of lifting the veil of arbitrariness and idiosyncrasy from metrical interpretations so that we can know in direct terms where we can
agree and how much must be left to taste.

Interest in the apparent preoccupation of the Middle Ages with
number symbolism has blossomed in recent years. Although it was
regular practice to note the poets' explicit statements of obviously
meaningful numbers, scholarship has now taken to minute calculation
of the length and composition of works and parts of works and even of
the number of syllables in a courtly poem. This has evoked the un-
thinking, negative reaction of some, and it is therefore especially welcome that Professor Batts has given us an excellent critical bibliography
of his subject in addition to his thoughtful survey of the state of the art.

This symposium volume has a lasting value beyond the oral performance of its contributors, but the spirit of keen excitement among the
participants and the lively give-and-take of views in the informal discussion groups and private exchanges will also be long remembered.
Then, too, there was a vital exemplification of the art of the troubadour
in the performance of Karl Wolfram. It is therefore fitting that the
song of Rumslant von Sachsen (*Jenaer Liederhandschrift* fol. 55b) and
the etching of the lutanist-singer (attributed to Israel van Meckenen,d.
1527) which embellished the programs of the symposium events
should appear on the cover of this book.

minnesang–performance and interpretation

BY RONALD J. TAYLOR

Surveying the research of the last hundred years or so, one might be forgiven for remarking that the disclosure of the full content and meaning of the *Minnesang* has been characterized by a certain reluctance. Pioneers like Bodmer in the eighteenth century and Tieck in the nineteenth concerned themselves only with the texts of the songs that they copied and published; early critical editors like Lachmann and Moriz Haupt did the same; alone among the great early figures in the history of German medieval scholarship, Friedrich Heinrich von der Hagen stands out as the man who gave, in the fourth volume of his *Minnesänger*, samples of the music that belonged to the texts and facsimiles of certain of the manscript sources in which this music was found. We may smile today at the early-nineteenth-century idiom of the piano accompaniments in his edition, but the fact remains that they are the product of an intention to provide an experience of whole songs, words and music, and not just of poems alone.

The nineteenth century subsequently witnessed sporadic attempts to deal with the music, but it is probably only from the time of Hugo Riemann, at the very end of the century, that one can date the existence of systematic musicological investigation into the principles underlying the art of the minnesinger. In the last fifty years the subject has attracted an ever-growing amount of attention, and through phonograph recordings by singers such as Hugues Cuénod and performances of works such as *The Play of Daniel*, medieval music has come to enjoy something of a vogue among the cultured public. It is certainly true to say that on the subject of the interpretation and performance of medieval music there is more evidence at our disposal today than ever before—though the pronouncement of a final verdict based on this evidence is no less hazardous than it ever was.

There is one further point I should like to make in this introductory historical context—and it is a point that is vital to our subject. However close we may come, whether unwittingly or by inspired scholarship, to

a true historical vision of the *Minnesang,* we cannot but feel and interpret its appeal as men of the twentieth century. That is to say, when we
hear this music we cannot dissociate from our auditory experience our
awareness of the music of the centuries that lie between the Middle
Ages and our own day. Our experience is a unique act of creativity, medieval in inspiration but contemporary in understanding and execution,
and because of its very contemporaneity, this act of creativity—which
strictly speaking does not, perhaps, have the status of a work of art but
is essentially akin to one—cannot but change the shape of the past.
There is a relevance to our concern in the words of T. S. Eliot in his
essay "Tradition and the Individual Talent":

> What happens when a new work of art is created is something that happens
> simultaneously to all the works of art which preceded it . . . . The existing
> order is complete before the new work arrives; for order to persist after the
> supervention of novelty, the *whole* existing order must be, if ever so slightly,
> altered . . . . Whoever has approved this idea of order . . . will not find it
> preposterous that the past should be altered by the present as much as the
> present is directed by the past.

By the same token we cannot, by some supreme act of imaginative re-
creation, induce in our minds the modes of appreciation which conditioned the minds of those twelfth- and thirteenth-century audiences
who first heard these songs. No doubt there were different kinds of
aesthetic experience to be enjoyed, and different people will have felt
different emotional responses to the songs performed in their presence.
And that a particular melody may be preserved, not just in one but in
several manuscripts, may indicate the wide currency and popularity of
that song. But where the source of its popularity lay, or what reactions
were released by its individual identifiable features, or what was
expected of a given song in a given situation, we cannot hope to know.
And therefore we can never feel as that first public felt.

Thus although it is possible to refine one's historical sense, one's
emotional and aesthetic responses, immediate by nature and conditioned by historical awareness, remain the responses of modern men.
Whatever the propriety of using old instruments for performing old
music, and however skillfully we may reconstruct these instruments for

present-day performance, we cannot hear the sounds of harp and flute, psaltery and dulcimer, as the men of the Middle Ages heard them. And since, we may note in passing, this is an aesthetic argument of general validity, it has its relevance, not only to the music with which we are here concerned, but also to our appreciation of the music of the Renaissance, the Baroque, and any other age from which we are separated by a considerable and decisive span of time. By all means let us play eighteenth-century continuo parts on the harpsichord rather than on the pianoforte. But let us at the same time also realize the nature of what we are doing.

The views that I should like to put forward in this essay can be divided into two parts—the one analytical and interpretative, the other practical and re-creative, corresponding to the two sides from which the *Minnesang,* or indeed any musical composition, has naturally to be considered. On the one hand lies our understanding of the composer's intentions and of the technical means by which he has sought to realize them; on the other lies the practical application of our understanding to the task of converting these intentions into living works of art.

A convenient way, I think, of approaching the first, the theoretical, aspect will be to try to reconstruct the way or ways in which the minnesinger could set about his task.

Customarily, but by no means invariably, both the words and the music of a song are the work of one and the same man. Usually the text of at least the first strophe of the poem, or the first *Spruch* in a particular *Ton,* appears to have been written before the melody; in other cases a poem is known to have been written to a pre-existing melody, sometimes composed by the poet himself, sometimes by another. The central consideration here, as in any situation where different arts are joined in a common enterprise, is that the one or the other art will assume the ascendancy at any given moment: in other words, that in a given work, or in the corpus of a particular artist, either the message of the text, or the strophic form of the poem, or the melodic and formal felicities of the melody, will appear to have had the greatest claim on his mind and ability, and thus to have flourished at the expense of its fellows. There is, for example, much labored and mediocre *Spruchdichtung* in the *Jenaer Liederhandschrift* by poets of little originality; at the same time there are many very accomplished melodies, stamped with the mark of distinguishable musical personalities.

That there should be this fluctuating and uneven balance between the constituent elements of a song is not unnatural. On the one side it reflects the disposition of artistic forces within the individual artist—that is, whether he is, or feels himself to be, a better poet than a composer, or more a self-conscious manipulator of formal techniques than an urgent preacher of ethical ideals. On the other side it may correspond to the different natures and purposes of different songs. For instance, the albeit incomplete melody to Walther von der Vogel-weide's *Sprüche* in the so-called Zweiter Philippston (18,15) has a conventional, almost perfunctory air about it which stands in contrast to the vital and highly personal tone of the texts. Conversely, while most of the strophes of Walther's famous *Palästinalied* (14,38) express a series of pious commonplaces on stock religious subject-matter, the solemn melody has a grave dignity that makes it one of the most moving of all medieval monodies. To balance the one aspect against the other, as the minnesinger himself must have done, is one of the tasks required of us as interpreters of his art.

The analytical and interpretative aspect of our research must therefore be carried on from three points of view: that of the text alone, that of the melody alone, and that of the interplay, conceptual and formal, of these two. It is often, indeed, in this third sphere—a dimension composed of natural correspondences but also of calculated tensions and oppositions—that the deepest interest and fullest pleasure of a song lie.

This is not the place for an exposé of the metrical skills of the minnesinger as such. But it is perhaps worth remarking that where an artist has lavished great care on the construction of his poem, employing refinements of line length, strophic proportion, and rhyme scheme, the accompanying music is often dull and characterless. Perhaps it is natural that a poet who makes it a paramount concern to indulge in elaborate wordplays and metrical sophistications should be unlikely to be able, or even to want, to match his verbal skill with a comparable musical skill, and that it should be in essence for a technical poetic achievement that he is remembered.

Illustrative examples of this are the Middle High German *Leiche* that have survived with both text and music. To compose a *Leich* is from the beginning to commit oneself to the performance of a tour de force. The succession of lyric versicles, each with its own metrical pattern, demands considerable ingenuity from the poet, and if it is true that in many *Leiche* the ability to sustain the quality of thought flags perceptibly toward the end, then it is even truer that the level of musical inventiveness often sinks distressingly low as the composer takes refuge in meaningless repetition. And if, under the pressure of the extended exercise, it is the metrical aspect of the *Gesamtkunstwerk* which appears to retain its individuality longest, it seems reasonable to infer that it is to this that the poet devoted the greater part of his creative skill.

We must, of course, not overlook the fact—which is of pervasive importance in the discussion, not only of this but also of all other aspects of the *Minnesang* as a musicopoetic entity—that we are far better informed about the poetry than about the music. We possess only one large codex—the *Jenaer Liederhandschrift*—which is coeval and comparable with the great *Liederhandschriften* of poems alone, and this contains an unfortunately large proportion of nondescript poems by Middle and Low German *Spruchdichter* who are not known to us from any other source. We have no original melodies by such key figures as Morungen and Reinmar, and a mere handful by Walther von der Vogelweide; not until the generation of Neidhart von Reuenthal do we strike the foundations of a substantial *Überlieferung* that affords us enough evidence to pronounce with reasonable certainty on basic questions of musical intent and character.

The transmission of music, particularly secular music, in the Middle Ages depended primarily on an oral rather than a written tradition, which is probably one of the most important reasons for the comparative paucity of written records. In consequence we are rarely in a position to make statements about the music of the *Minnesang* with such certainty as we are about the poetry—which has not, however, prevented a large number of people from doing so. Although, for example, we are able through the apparatus of textual criticism, to examine closely and extensively the poetic techniques of minnesingers from the Golden Age of medieval German literature, and to isolate their poetic personalities, we have far fewer opportunities to perform the same service for their melodies. How, then, can we characterize the tunes known to us so that we may build up the composite picture of our interpretation? Most usefully, I think, under two aspects: the one, that of melodic content and idiom, the other, that of form.

Even a casual acquaintance with the songs of the minnesingers—and the same is true of the songs of the troubadours and the trouvères—reveals that the melodic vocabulary of many of them is drawn from the language of Gregorian chant. The *Palästinalied* of Walther von der Vogelweide is as good an example of this as one could wish for.[1] Many minnesingers of the class of *ministerialis*—Walther, Reinmar, and Neidhart among them—certainly received a formal education in the seven liberal arts at a monastery school and, quite apart from the content of the arid mathematical discipline of *musica,* could not have failed to experience there the music that accompanied the acts of devotion and worship. It would indeed be surprising if some of the characteristics of this music had not rubbed off on men, albeit of secular interests and callings, who came within its ambience. The use of the Dorian mode, of melismatic flourishes, and of certain formal turns of melody, especially in the cadences, surely owes its presence in these songs to the monastic surroundings in which the authors received their formal education.

At the same time, however, we find ourselves confronted with melodies in what we would call in modern terms a major key, melodies that comparative research has shown to be independent of the ecclesiastical melodic modes of plainchant and proper to an autonomous secular tradition. This dichotomy has social implications that cannot be pursued here, but it also has an intrinsic musical significance that bears directly upon the question of performance and is thus vital to the whole

[1] See Ronald J. Taylor, *The Art of the Minnesinger* (Cardiff, 1968), Vol. I, pp. 95–96, and Vol. II, pp. 142 ff.

question of interpretation. For through the recognition of separate musical traditions, the one ecclesiastical, the other secular, to both of which the minnesinger of noble birth or of *ministerialis* rank was by his social position exposed, we provide an important contextual framework for our historical interpretation of the art of *Minnesang*.

From the characterization of melody the argument leads to the characterization of formal structure. This is a confused and confusing chapter in our knowledge, and the primary source of confusion, I am tempted to say, lies in the attempts of scholars to see, in the diverse patterns of melodic phrases, structures and symmetries that are not really there.

This is not to say that these songs are formless. Indeed, when one considers the subtleties with which the minnesingers invested their poetic texts, it would be something of an incongruity to find that the musical content was amorphous and unplanned. But at the same time it is hardly possible to deny that an ability, and perhaps desire, to compose and arrange melodic phrases in such elaborate, not to say self-conscious, ways is far less apparent. We shall look in vain for an ordered formal balance such as that which informs the symphony and the fugue. The means by which meaningful musical form is created—such as the recapitulation of phrases or groups of phrases, modulation, and transposition—are certainly to be found, but their employment seems to be more random than calculated, more the product of chance and whim than of a deliberate architectonic view of the task of composition. To act on the assumption that there must always be such an act of over-all planning, in the sense in which we use the term today, can only lead one to bend the historical evidence into patterns to which one feels it ought to conform. The urge toward categorization and schematization which dominates so much discussion of the form of the *Minnesang* seems to me, however understandable, to be misplaced and unreal in the face of the actual musical evidence as it lies before us.

Yet at the same time there *are* signs in these melodies of what might be called directions or tendencies of form. A common example is a tripartite construction in which the third section consists, in part, of the recapitulation, sometimes exact, sometimes with modifications, of melodic material from the first section. The recapitulation may be

simply of the last phrase of the *Stollen* melody, producing a symmetrical rounding-off of the *Aufgesang* and the *Abgesang* with the
same musical material, as in Walther's *Palästinalied*; sometimes two or
three phrases, possibly with variants and decorations, may be re-
capitulated in this way.[2]

In contrast to this tendency, which betokens a total view, however
modest, of the melodic phrases covering the song, we find a form of
piecemeal development in which individual phrases or even isolated
handfuls of notes are taken and subjected to a succession of random
repetitions and developments. This "zerstückelte Entwicklung" can
lead to a situation in which a strophe of, say, ten lines is met by a mere
three or four basic melodic phrases which, either in their entirety or in
separate parts, are repeated, augmented, diminished, and otherwise
developed in a completely free manner so as to cover all ten lines of
the text.[3]

Allied to this is the rondo principle, in which one main phrase
alternates with a series of usually unrelated subsidiary phrases. There
is something immediate, spontaneous, about this style of composition
in that the composer does not appear to think more than a phrase or
two ahead but to move in an almost improvisatory manner, letting one
phrase suggest the course of the next. It does, in a humble way, reflect
a desire to provide formal links between individual phrases, but,
equally, it is far from implying a total formal view, a structural balance
over the song as a whole. It is hard to see, in the present state of our
knowledge, that we can do much more than describe objectively and
soberly the state of affairs with which the manuscripts present us,
resisting the temptation to systematize where it cannot be proven that
there is a system. Wherever the political sympathies of the medievalist
editor and scholar may lie, conservatism is a virtue not to be under-
estimated in his scholarly policies and actions.

It is interesting to observe that there appear to be no perceptible

---

[2] Cf., among many others, songs 9, 10, and 13 of Der Meissner (*Jenaer
Liederhandschrift* fol. 91c, 91d, and 94a).

[3] A striking example of this kind of composition is Neidhart's song 11 (see
A. T. Hatto and R. J. Taylor, *The Songs of Neidhart von Reuental,* Manchester
[1958], pp. 32 and 95).

correspondences between the nature or purpose of individual poems and the melodies set to those poems. One cannot observe, for example, that a religious *Spruch* is always accompanied by a melody derivated from Church music. Similarly there is to love song, political *Spruch,* dawn song, or other distinguishable genre of medieval lyrical poetry no single corresponding melodic type that came to be regarded as the appropriate equivalent to the sentiment of the text. Nor did the Middle Ages distinguish, by "modern" ethical criteria, between properly religious music and a secular music that could not be tolerated in Church circles: a folk tune might be incorporated as a *canto fermo* in a setting of the Mass, as with Christopher Tye's use of the English folk song "The Western Wind," and the question of appropriateness would not arise. And, indeed, church buildings themselves in the Middle Ages were often the scene of activities more appropriate to the market place and the tavern than to the House of God.

If now, to conclude this consideration of interpretation and typology, we place analysis of poems alongside analysis of melodies, we obtain an interesting picture of independences and interrelationships. In general there is a broad pattern of correspondences between the outlines of the metrical and the musical forms: in other words, a phrase of melody generally coincides with a line of text, so that a strophe of, say, eight lines is usually covered by a parallel set of eight melodic phrases, however independent of the arrangement of the melodic phrases the strophic disposition of line lengths, rhymes, and so on may be.

But at the same time there are not a few songs in which the metrical and musical schemes, far from being the natural complement of one another, are arranged so as to produce a series of tensions. One of the commonest ways of doing this is to put against two text lines of four stresses each a musical phrase of five bars plus one of three. The compound unit is one of eight bars, but the text and the music fill these eight bars in different ways. We even have songs whose texts are in the familiar tripartite form of *Stollen* + *Stollen* + *Abgesang* but whose melodies ride roughshod over the parallelism of the two *Stollen* and cover the text of the complete *Aufgesang* with a succession of unrelated phrases.[4] It is in such songs that we find some of the most interesting examples of the minnesinger's sense of form within the two artistic fields in which he was working, poetry and music. Once again we find ourselves confronted, as did the minnesinger himself, with the rival claims of two arts. It is the manner of the reconciliation of these claims which provides us with the raw materials of our exercises in interpretation.

How, then, building on this theoretical basis of interpretation, are we to approach the practical task of performance? For we must not forget that the songs of the minnesinger were composed for performance, not for study, and existed as sounds in the minds of diverse audiences before they were recorded on parchment and paper. The existence of this oral tradition is of particular importance for the study of the manuscript sources themselves, and although this is a subject that cannot occupy us here, it is a consideration not to be lost sight of in the context of performance from these sources.

As they are preserved, and with such obvious exceptions as the polyphonic songs of Oswald von Wolkenstein, the melodies of minnesinger songs, like those of the troubadours and trouvères, are recorded as single lines of melody, without accompaniment. If we were to take this state of affairs at its face value, we would conclude that the songs were sung as pure monody, with no accompaniment of any kind. By the same logic we might also have to conclude that, since the overwhelming majority of our manuscript sources contain poems but no melodies, the texts were recited and not sung—or, even more drastic, that melodies had never been written to them at all.

But we are fortunately not at the utter mercy of this dubious logic. In the fifteenth-century Berlin codex germ. fol. 922,[5] for example, there are songs in which far more notes are recorded than the syllables of the text can possibly cover, and after phrases have been allocated to all the lines of the poem, the remaining notes may well be regarded as instrumental preludes, interludes, or postludes. If this is the correct

---

[4] A particularly interesting example of the interplay of textual and musical form is the song by Wizlav von Rügen in the *Jenaer Liederhandschrift* fol. 76b.

[5] See Margarete Lang, *Zwischen Minnesang und Volkslied* (Berlin, 1941).

interpretation, it would testify to the reality of the situation in which an instrument made its contribution to the song along with the voice part. At the same time, even granted the possibility of this interpretation, one cannot extrapolate from this one example to the corpus of *Minnesang* at large.

There are, however, other sources from which we can cull information on the subject. One is the literature of the time, which is rich in descriptions of music-making by different kinds of musicians and in a variety of social settings. The range of musical instruments available on festive occasions in court circles, for example, is colorfully described by Hartmann in his account of the wedding of Erec and Enite (*Erec*, lines 2150 ff.). In a different context, the performance of epic lays by a solo singer is described in Gottfried's *Tristan*[6] and also, in greater detail, in the thirteenth-century French epic known as the *Chanson de Horn*.[7] From these sources we learn that the singer used a stringed instrument—in the former case a harp, in the latter, a fiddle—to accompany himself.

This is, of course, epic material, but the distinction, for our present purposes, between strophic epic on the one hand and lyric on the other is not as strict as might be imagined. The most illuminating piece of evidence that links the two genres is the melody to the verse epic known as the *Jüngerer Titurel* (the melody is transcribed in my *The Art of the Minnesinger,* vol. I, pp. 107–108; see also Commentary, vol. II, pp. 164–166). Whether this melody is that composed by Wolfram to his own *Titurel* or whether it is the work of his continuator Albrecht von Scharfenberg is immaterial: in metrical form the strophe, which is allied with that of the *Nibelungenlied* and *Kudrun,* lies historically closer to the earliest forms of Middle High German sung lyric—Kürenberg, Meinloh von Sevelingen—than any exclusively lyric forms of a later generation. And the melody presents no features that are not to be found in the stock of *Minnesang* melodies proper. Further-

[6] Gottfried von Strassburg, *Tristan und Isold*, ed. Friedrich Ranke (Berlin, 1930), lines 3624 ff.

[7] *The Romance of Horn*, ed. Mildred K. Pope, vol. I (Oxford, 1955), p. 97. See also the useful commentary with translation of lines 2830–2843 in vol. II (Oxford, 1964), p. 155. (Anglo-Norman Texts, IX–X; XII–XIII).

more there occurs at the halfway point of the melody, and again at the end, a melismatic group of notes which is not taken up by the words of the text and may well be interpreted as an instrumental interjection between groups of sung phrases—which would recall the situation in the Berlin codex germ. fol. 922, to which I referred earlier, and also the manner of performance described in the *Chanson de Horn.*

In the realm of Middle High German lyric poetry we have, for instance, the accounts by Tannhäuser of the enthusiastic instrumental support given to the performance of his *Tanzleiche*: on one occasion, according to Tannhäuser, the fiddler broke a string, and on another, so abandoned did the musical proceedings become, he even snapped his bow.[8] We might well recall these occasions when we sit down in our genteel drawing rooms to listen with earnest mien and keen historical acumen to refined and delicate recitals of this music.

Literary evidence on this question may also reside in the use by certain poets of technical or semitechnical terms in their descriptions of music-making. Thus the verbs "discantieren" and "organieren," which are found in Gottfried von Strassburg, Oswald von Wolkenstein, and others, refer to polyphonic practices; and when Gottfried says admiringly of Walther von der Vogelweide, "wie spaehe s'organieret!"[9] he is testifying, as Burdach pointed out many years ago,[10] to Walther's skill in adding a second, accompanimental musical part to the melody of his songs and thereby revealing that the *Minnesang* was, or could be, performed with a contrapuntal or harmonic accompaniment. In the next breath, unfortunately, we have to admit that, since no such accompaniment is written into the manuscript, we have no record of what it consisted of.

Two allied sources of information are the sculpture of the Middle Ages and the illustrative decoration in manuscripts of both secular and religious content. In both these realms we find portrayals of figures singing and accompanying themselves on a fiddle or a harp. Moreover,

[8] J. Siebert, *Der Dichter Tannhäuser* (Halle, 1934), pp. 94 and 99.

[9] Gottfried von Strassburg, *Tristan,* line 4803.

[10] Kurt Plenio, "Bausteine zur altdeutschen Strophik," *PBB* 42 (1917), p. 445, n. 3.

from the way in which they handle the instruments, and from the appearance of the instruments themselves, we can gain impressions of what sounds could be produced—but this is of course not the same as knowing that such sounds really were produced. On the basis of this pictorial evidence modern reproductions have been made for purposes of performance—though once again we cannot know how the sounds we make on such instruments today relate to those made in the thirteenth century.

The points I have made so far provide, I think, sufficient evidence for the existence of the practice of the instrumental accompaniment of the secular songs of the Middle Ages, whether sung by a solo singer or intended for communal performance. This does not imply, however, that all songs were necessarily accompanied in this way, or that those that could have been so accompanied, always were. On the contrary, it seems reasonable to assume that most minnesinger songs were performed in a variety of ways, the particular way at a particular moment depending on the nature of the occasion, the constitution of the musical forces available, and probably also on the taste and whim of the man who was directing the performance. Certain of the more distinctively personal songs may well have been sung by a soloist alone: *we* feel that it would be more appropriate so, but there is no proof that the Middle Ages felt the same way. On the other hand, dance songs, or *Sprüche* of generalized didactic intent, might well belong in a community setting where those present, men and women, took part according to the measure of their desire and their ability—singing; playing a stringed, wind, or percussion instrument; or simply moving in sympathy with the music.

Yet even if one concedes that these and other forms of accompaniment were in fact practiced, there still remains the problem of what precisely, in actual notes, the accompaniment consisted of, since the manuscripts record nothing of it. And, after all, if we are to attempt to perform these songs today—remembering that they were composed for the ear, not for the eye—our performances must both stand the test of aesthetic adequacy and bear the scrutiny of historical scholarship. Thus I would like to conclude by offering a few practical observations on this issue, acknowledging the claims, as I understand them, of both the historical and the aesthetic standpoints and seeking to draw attention to what appears to offer a reasonable basis for modern performance.

First, I think that we cannot ignore the possibility, raised by the nature of the manuscripts themselves, that as early as the thirteenth century there prevailed, at least in certain German courts, the custom of reciting the texts as poems rather than singing them as songs. To be sure, one cannot say that, just because in a certain manuscript the texts are recorded without the melodies, these texts were meant to be recited and not sung, for we possess songs that are preserved in one source with melody and in another without. Yet the overwhelming predominance of nonmusical sources does lead one to suspect that the melodies mattered less to German patrons than the texts. This is a situation somewhat different, though not radically so, from that which obtains in the realm of the troubadours and trouvères, about whose music we are considerably better informed—though here, too, there are considerably more manuscripts extant of texts alone than of texts and melodies together.

If we assume a musical performance, however, we should take as our starting point the vital division of medieval monodies into those that derive from Gregorian chant and thus bear the mark of ecclesiastical provenance and those that belong to the world of what we are pleased to call the "modern" major scale, which is of secular origin and has no historical place among the Church modes—and is, moreover, far from "modern."

On one side of the dividing line, as I mentioned earlier, lie the melodies composed in the idiom of Gregorian chant. One of the essential and inalienable qualities of Gregorian melodies is that they are pure melodic structures. They are not composed according to any latent harmonic principles, and by their nature they resist accompaniment or other treatment in harmonic terms. That such an accompaniment is provided in celebrations of the Catholic Mass today does not invalidate this law; in fact all but the most subtle and tasteful such accompaniments prove how valid it is. These accompaniments represent an inevitable but regrettable concession to the force of our Western musical consciousness, which for historical reasons can hardly help but

hear a melody in terms of the harmonic framework that has governed
the evolution of our musical experience.

Therefore, just as plainchant melodies should by nature be kept free
from harmonic accompaniment, so also, by the same nature, should
these medieval secular monodies that are drawn from the world of
plainchant. A song that may have been intended for communal partici-
pation, such as a song of pilgrimage or crusade, could have had a
rhythmical accompaniment on percussion instruments or by clapping;
there might also be some vocal or instrumental embellishment of the
melodic line itself by singers or instrumentalists other than the princi-
pal performer. But anything approaching what we would call harmony
would be alien to the idiom.

With tunes in the major mode, on the other hand, the situation is
quite the reverse. The major mode, with the harmonic framework
latent in it, is the basis of the music of the Western world. And although there are isolated European examples of it before the twelfth
century, it is in the secular corpus of troubadour, trouvère, and minnesinger music that we find the first substantial group of major melodies.
Taken together, these two facts convey the historical importance that
attaches to these songs and reveal the historical continuity that confronts
us when we deal with them.

The possibility, therefore—one might even say the inevitability—of
a harmonic accompaniment to *Minnesang* melodies in a major mode is
the most important and most fascinating realization in the matter of
performance. I have already quoted some of the historical evidence for
the use of the fiddle in the accompaniment of medieval singing. The
fiddle of the twelfth and thirteenth centuries usually had between four
and six strings, one of which often bypassed the bridge and served as
a drone; moreover, as can be seen from German and French illustra-
tions and sculptures (see frontispiece),[11] the bridge itself remained flat
as late as the fourteenth century, so that it would have been difficult to
bow the inner strings individually in order to play a melodic line;
perhaps it was not even intended that they should be so bowed. The
introduction of the curved bridge, of course, is what makes this pos-

[11] Cf., for example, the illustration at the head of the poems of Reinmar der
Fiedler in the *Manessische Liederhandschrift* fol. 312ro.

sible and what marks the beginning of the history of the violin as a lyrical melodic instrument.

This is not to say that no form of melodic playing was possible on the medieval fiddle: the outer strings could be freely bowed and stopped, or the bow could be discarded and the individual strings plucked in the manner of a guitar. Literary sources, too, make it clear that tunes *were* played on the fiddle. But it still appears true that, by its basic shape and method of construction, one—if not *the*—natural mode of performance would have been to draw the bow across two or more of the strings simultaneously and thus to produce an accompaniment, however crude, that was essentially, though primitively, harmonic.

We must remember also that the cultivation of instrumental playing in the Middle Ages was overwhelmingly a secular concern. Certain of the early Church fathers, St. Jerome among them, saw the playing of instruments as a threat to the purity of the religious spirit and warned the faithful against exposing themselves to the evil worldly influence. Pagan dance festivals no doubt bore some responsibility for this attitude, and the association of instrumental music with such occasions led to suspicion, amounting to condemnation, of all such music. It is ironical to note, in passing, that the influence of this secular music seeped into the music of the Church itself through the practice of *musica ficta,* or *musica falsa,* by which chromatic alterations were made to certain notes of the ecclesiastical modes in certain melodic progressions, drawing the musical idiom toward that of the major mode.

The final piece of information in this argument linking the major mode, the realm of instrumental music, and the secular tradition is provided by the natural laws of acoustics. The upper partials of the so-called harmonic series produce, after the octave and the fifth, first the notes of the major triad, and then, one by one, the notes of the major scale. This means that, for example, the simple, unkeyed wind instruments of the Middle Ages, such as the shawm and the recorder, produced by their very nature melodies in the major mode—a fact of which certain learned medieval theorists of music showed themselves to be fully aware.[12]

[12] Johannes de Garlandia (early thirteenth century): "Videndum est de

To conclude these remarks, and to point the argument with a specific example, I cite the famous Provençal song "Kalenda maya." The chronicle[13] tells how two minstrels came to the court of the Marquis Boniface II at Montferrat and played a tune on their fiddles. The melody so caught the fancy of the Marquis's sister that she asked the troubadour Raimbaut de Vacqueiras, who was also of the company, to write a poem to it. He did so, the result being the May song "Kalenda maya." And the tune is in the key of C major.

I have attempted in these remarks to assemble some suggestions on the performance and interpretation of the *Minnesang* which are both supported by the documentation of history and acceptable to the criteria of aesthetics. Undeniably, many doubts persist, and an exclusive, all-embracing certainty is not, and never will be, within our grasp. But the challenge remains—and there is no alibi for faintheartedness.

---

musica falsa que instrumentis musicalibus multum est necessaria." in: C. de Coussemaker, *Scriptorum de musica medii aevi nova series,* [Paris 1864–1876], vol. 1, p. 166.

[13] C. Chabaneau, *Les biographies des troubadours en langue provençale* (Toulouse, 1885), p. 87 f.

mınnesang and the form of performance

BY HUGO KUHN

$\mathcal{A}$s early as the last stage but one of *Minnesang* research, exemplified in the monumental lifework of Carl von Kraus, scholars had turned away completely from the biographical approach of the nineteenth century. Together with the "history of ideas," formal, literary-critical, and aesthetic considerations determined the image of *Minnesang* anew, down to text criticism itself, and perhaps excessively there. The melodies that unfortunately are so rarely extant for German minnesongs, the work required to uncover and disclose them, and their interpretation by structural categories contributed a great deal that was new even at that time.[1] The content of *Minnesang*—in other words, *minne* itself—was no longer interpreted biographically but artistically. For Carl von Kraus, *minne* became artistically varied "positions" of the experience of love, if you will forgive the physiological ring, positions that were discussed in deep reflection, used polemically, and combined into cycles. Despite this, however, *minne* retained, as the example of von Kraus once more shows, a fateful and even fatal note of experience lyrics. Viewed biographically, Reinmar the Elder could, after all, still function as an example of the *grande passion* and of its literary history from ancient Egypt up to Stendhal and Tolstoy. When, however, his poetry is interpreted as merely a fictional experience, as a play with words of love—even if that word was "bîligen"—the loss is lamentable.

The most recent phase of *Minnesang* research, as it is characterized to my great pleasure, particularly by this symposium, appears, viewed externally, to stay completely within the framework of that last phase but one. Where it does not, it may destroy as many clear insights as it provides new ones through statistics and interpretation of metrical and

NOTE—Translated by Stanley N. Werbow.

[1] Walther von der Vogelweide, *Die Gedichte,* ed. K. Lachman, 13th edition ed. H. Kuhn on the basis of the 10th edition of Carl von Kraus (Berlin, 1965). I am indebted to Dr. Christoph Petzsch for technical and bibliographic help.

strophic structures (even including interpretations based on number symbolism), interpretation of the rhythm and melodics of the melodies, and study of the rhetoric of the texts of the poems. We still have a great deal to expect from recent research on the poems of the fourteenth and fifteenth century (Stackmann, Kibelka, Petzsch).[2] Viewed more deeply, however, the point of departure of that penultimate epoch has already been abandoned and a new one, covering all aspects of *Minnesang*, is in sight. I name no names and cite no examples, because, poor victim of the German "University Industry" that I am, I might very well have overlooked important and characteristic items, particularly from the United States, and this symposium is sign enough of the new orientation.

My purpose is to reconcile the various formal and artistic aspects of *Minnesang* with its content, that is, with the *minne* problem itself. In this connection, one hitherto neglected formal aspect seems helpful, namely, the fact that the forms and word sequences of the *minne* songs reveal their full meaning and life only in the living situation of the minnesong as it is performed by the singer. We shall not concern ourselves with whether these forms were pristine and unique with the poet-singer or whether in the process of repetition by him and others they crystallized into the extant written text. According to the art historian Dagobert Frey, every artistic creation of the Middle Ages should be regarded not so much as a finished, simultaneous form, as it is in modern times, but as a successive unfolding of that form. However, even if the form of the song in the Middle Ages must be understood as successive—that is, as a process of melodic and metrical song-formation and thought development—the situation of this successive process, the "performance" of the song, is nevertheless a further vital

---

[2] K. Stackmann, *Der Spruchdichter Heinrich von Mügeln. Vorstudien zur Erkenntnis seiner Individualität* (Probleme der Dichtung. Studien zur deutschen Literaturgeschichte 3) (Heidelberg, 1958). J. Kibelka, *Der ware meister. Denkstile und Bauformen in der Dichtung Heinrichs von Mügeln* (Philologische Studien und Quellen 13) (Berlin, 1963). C. Petzsch, "Studien zum Meistergesang des Hans Folz," *DVjs* 36 (1962), 190–247; "Text- und Melodietypveränderung bei Oswald von Wolkenstein," *DVjs* 38 (1964), 491–512; "Text-Form-Korrespondenzen im mittelalterlich Strophenlied," *DVjs* 41 (1967), 27–60.

point of view for form and content. I choose as an example only one song, but one which is assuredly the most basic in theme and form in all German *Minnesang*—the so-called crusade song of Hartmann von Aue, *Minnesangs Frühling* 218,5:

218,5   Ich var mit iuwern hulden, herren unde mage:
        liut unde lant diu müezen saelic sin.
        es ist unnot daz iemen miner verte vrage:
        ich sage wol für war die reise min.
        mich vienc diu Minne und lie mich vri uf mine sicherheit.
10   nu hat si mir enboten bi ir liebe daz ich var.
        ez ist unwendic: ich muoz endelichen dar:
        wie kume ich braeche mine triuwe und minen eit!
            Sich rüemet manger waz er dur die Minne taete:
        wa sint diu werc? die rede hoere ich wol.
15   doch saehe ich gerne dazs ir eteslichen baete
        daz er ir diente als ich ir dienen sol.
        ez ist geminnet, der sich dur die Minne ellenden muoz.
        nu seht wies mich uz miner zungen ziuhet über mer.
        und lebt min herre, Salatin und al sin her
20   dienbraehten mich von Vranken niemer einen fuoz.
            Ir minnesinger, iu muoz ofte misselingen:
        daz iu den schaden tuot daz ist der wan.
        ich wil mich rüemen, ich mac wol von minne singen,
        sit mich diu minne hat und ich si han.
25   daz ich da wil, seht daz wil alse gerne haben mich:
        so müezt ab ir verliesen under wilen wanes vil:
        ir ringent umbe liep daz iuwer niht enwil:
        wan mügt ir armen minnen solhe minne als ich?

This poem has had extraordinary interest for scholars almost exclusively on account of the opportunity for dating which lines 19 and 20 appear to provide, an opportunity which text-critical controversies stubbornly refuse to allow to be used definitively. This disputed passage need by no means occupy us unduly. Nor do I intend to go into the metrics and strophic structure, or into the melody, which is not extant. Viewed on a formal basis, these are relatively easy to comprehend in the framework of the "French" phase of German *Minnesang*. Since I do not wish to give a full explication of this poem here, I do not adduce the numerous contributions of scholarship; they have been taken into account. I am interested only in the matter of the performance format of the poem and the thematic implications of that.

It begins: "Ich var . . . ," a song and perhaps a topos common throughout the Middle Ages—for example, in the pilgrims' song: "In gotes namen varen wir . . .";[3] in the love song of the fifteenth century: "Ich var dahin wan es muss sein . . ."[4] Even *Minnesang* utilizes this formula; the beginning of Morungen's song: "Ich wil eine reise, wünschet daz ich wol gevar . . ." (*MF* 145,33) is an almost exact parallel with Hartmann's, and even Walther (60,34)—"Ich wil nu teilen e ich var . . ."—is constructed upon the "Ich var" situation. But the concept "topos" does not appear to me to encompass all the essential aspects of these song beginnings. Another typical song beginning that was widespread in the Middle Ages is the formula of "good tidings" (*gute neue Mär*), which occurs throughout the whole Middle Ages, from Walther's "Song of Praise"—"Welcome me, for I bring you news" (56,14: *Ir sult sprechen willekomen, der iu maere bringet daz bin ich*)—to Luther's "I bring you good news from Heaven" (*Vom Himmel hoch da komm ich her, ich bring euch gute neue Mär*). Its situation is, so to speak, the role of the minstrel par excellence; the minstrel appears as a bringer of "new tidings" (*neue Zeitung*), as it is phrased in the sixteenth century, in a manner closer to our time and further from poetry.

[3] F. M. Böhme, *Altdeutsches Liederbuch* (Leipzig, 1877 [reprinted 1966]), no. 568. The note there discusses the early history of the formula and refers to Gottfried's *Tristan* (Ranke edition) 11533 f.: *und sungen eines unde zwir:/'in gotes namen varen wir.'* The phrase accordingly was known before the early thirteenth century; Böhme also provides a reprint of five renderings, three of them with melody, from the fifteenth and sixteenth centuries.

[4] *Lochamer Liederbuch* no. 8 (facs. ed. Konrad Ameln, 1925), written down about 1452; religious contrafacture (previously ?) in cgm 4702, which now contains only a religious text from 1444. Cf. C. Petzsch, "Der cgm 4702: Zwei frühe Kontrafakturen zum Lochamer-Liederbuch," *ZfdA* 92 (1963), 227–240.

In the fifteenth-century formulaic: *gesegn dich gott! Ich far dahin,* also the close of song 1568 of Hans Sachs (Stuttgart Litt. Verein vol. 207, p. 393). For the persistence of the formula, see also *ZfdPh* 26 (1894), 213.

"Ich var": Parting certainly has a general, human content, but it is more concrete in the song of the Middle Ages. The rest of the beginning of the song—". . . mit iuweren hulden, herren unde mage" (with your favor, lords and kinsmen)—extends the "Ich var" role by a well-known leave-taking formula. And the very next line—"may land and people be blessed" (*liut unde lant diu müezen saelic sin*)—adds a blessing formula at parting. However, the very next two lines—"no need for you to ask about my journey, I'll tell you the very truth about it now" (*es ist unnot, daz iemen miner verte vrage, ich sage wol für war die reise min*)—can be understood literally only as a highly refined continuation of the minstrel's act. Why is no one to ask the purpose and goal of the minstrel's journey off to war? Why does he propose to tell about it so expressly—"wol für war"—in order not to tell it at all but to present us with a puzzle: Love captured me" (*Mich vienc diu minne* [218,9])? The answer is that the poem, as its text proves and as research has unanimously assumed, is a religious call-up to a crusade, a well-known song type in Latin, French, and German for which a certain comprehension by the public could be expected. But, starting with this curious "prisoner of love" theme, it behaves in theme and word sequence just as plainly and one-sidedly as a secular love song, specifically a reflection on true *minne*, another type assured in advance of audience comprehension. The tension between the two genres and the thematic dialectic that results are what most precisely determines the form, the word choice, and the sequence of ideas of the whole structure.

How does this dialectic become plain to the listener? Not directly by the form and text of the song. The work takes on its wealth of allusion and significance only by drawing the explicit, secular *minne* theme into the unstated religious crusade theme. This latter, therefore, must be present and visible in the situation, in the "act" of the singer, and must be a part of the whole performance, even though unspoken. That is the significance and function of the "Ich var" role, and it requires precise representation of a departure for a crusade. Might not this representation be a cross on the garment of the departing one, a visible sign of this religious obligation? Thus the crusade theme, though not expressed in the text, is "announced" both in the formula and in the role of the minstrel and permits a dialectical play with the "minnesingers."

The situation that has been revealed in the first four lines becomes strangely enigmatic for the viewer and listener in the fifth line: "Mich vienc diu Minne und lie mich vri [MS. varn] uf mine sicherheit" (218,9) (Love captured me and set me free on my own surety). The crusade knight of the scene declares himself to be a prisoner of love.

The prisoner of love is not actually a topos of *Minnesang*. Hartmann uses the convention of the servant of love somewhat later in the poem (218,16) and, surprisingly enough, also addresses the *minne* poets themselves (218,21). But in the fourteenth and fifteenth centuries the prisoner of love becomes literally a graphic topos in the minne-slave cycles of frescoes and tapestries.[5] Nourished by the courtly epic and *novella*, artists portray Tristan, Wigalois, Solomon, and Aristotle and Phyllis as *minne* slaves. Hartmann, too, has taken over the *minne*-prisoner type from the epic into the song, which is not surprising: giving quarter upon condition is a very frequent situation in the courtly epic, in which a conquered opponent in an "adventure" is spared on his honor and is ordered as evidence of the adventure to report to his conqueror's mistress, who then has him at her disposal. That is precisely what happens in Hartmann's song in the very next line: "She has ordered me by her love, that I should go" (*Nu hat sie mir enboten bi ir liebe, daz ich var*). Scholarship is in complete agreement that by this is meant the mustering of a crusade army. After the participants have pledged themselves to go, after the cross has been sewn to the garment, then the muster is called. But a mustering up of a prisoner of love? And who is Hartmann's mistress in the song, "diu Minne," and what is "ir liebe"?

Taken literally as the second and third strophe employ the text dialectically, it is the *Minne* of the *minne* servant and minnesinger, in part a personified abstraction, in part a concretely evoked beloved. (It is that which provides the *pointe* of the final line, 218,25, and thus

[5] Friedrich Maurer, "Der Topos von den 'Minnesklaven'," *DVjs* 27 (1953) 182–206, with reproduction of the Malterer tapestry from the Augustinian museum in Freiburg im Breisgau.

the question whether *Minne* should be capitalized or not can scarcely be solved.) But within the framework of the crusade theme, which is present in the poem solely in the appearance of the singer and his wearing the sign of the cross, it is divine love—love of God, who "first loved us" (1 John 4:19)—from which the dialectic of mutual love in the third strophe is developed. Concretely present in the form of the cross on the garment, *Minne* is the Saviour himself in the land of his birth, life, death, and resurrection (cf. Walther 14,38), a land for the liberation of which from the heathens the crusader must travel "uz miner zungen . . . uber mer" (218,18). The conclusion of the first strophe strengthens our perception of the author's intention of irritating by means of this play between the double significance of the words of the song and the performance of the song: the inescapability of the crusade "thither" into the Holy Land and the religious and moral deepening of faith and obligation by oath (*triuwe unt eit*) are confirmed in an unspoken but visible manner, solely by the presence of the sign of the cross. However, the minnesong and *minne*-epic terminology continues to comprise the puzzle.

The second strophe picks up this moral and legal obligation in a religious sense but does it once again by apostrophizing *Minnesang*. Boasting, "sich rüemen" (218,13), is after all what *Minnesang* is, seen from the outside. That is the way the satirist Heinrich von Melk viewed it in its early days: "Swa sich diu ritterschaft gesamnet, da hebet sich ir wechselsage, wie manige der unt der behuret habe; ir laster mugen si nicht verswigen, ir ruom ist niwan von den wiben" (*Erinnerung an den Tod* 345 ff.) (Wherever Knights are gathered, they begin their talk back and forth, about how many this one or the other one has made a whore; they find it impossible to keep quiet about their vices; their boasting is only of women). And that is the way in which the *Spielmann* Gedrut (A) or Geltar (C) views high *Minnesang* in the thirteenth century: "you are much too fat with all your mourning complaint, if there were anything really to it and someone pined for love as you do, he would be dead in a year" (*ir sit ze veiz bi klagender not, waer ieman ernst der sich also nach minnen senet, der laeg inner jares friste tot* [KLD 13, I, 7 ff.]).

Here Hartmann indicts *Minnesang* crudely, viewed from the outside (as he also does, in his other criticism of *Minnesang* in poem 216,29, which does not have a religious basis), and he criticizes it as Gedrut-Geltar does with the Biblical words versus works formula (cf. 218,14). Then he quotes his own crusade and *minne* formula from the first strophe against *Minnesang* with a light, ironic tone when he says (218,15 f.): "Doch saehe ich gerne daz si [*die Minne*] ir eteslichen baete" (Yet I wish that love would bid some of them . . .)—compare 218,10: "nu hat sie mir enboten bi ir liebe" (now she has bid by her love)—"daz er ir diente als ich ir dienen sol" (that he might serve her as I do). A distinction in content, however, between the crusade *minne* and *Minnesänger minne,* between the love of God and love of woman, between divine and earthly love, is not made. Hartmann employs the imperious mistress *Minne* here as one and the same. Her service should therefore likewise be one and the same. And it is only in that way that his definition of *minne* proper has such powerful force: "ez ist geminnet, der sich dur die Minne ellenden muoz" (218,17) (he, and only he, practices true *minne,* who for the sake of *Minne* [of the abstraction and the person and upon her request, see strophe I] must go into exile, into foreign lands, into privation and self-denial, who must fare forth, "varn" in the sense of the situation of the song beginning).

What of "Sich ellenden" as a common measure for divine and earthly love, for love of God and love of woman? Going into exile is naturally seen on the one hand from the point of view of the minstrel's performance, the crusade apparently without any illusion[6] of secular success, simply as an obligation of religious *minne,* but *"ellenden"* also belongs perhaps to the secular "Ich var" formula. In the song "Innsbruck ich muss dich lassen ich var dahin mein Strassen . . . ,"[7] the first strophe ends with the words: "Wo ich im Elend bin." In

---

[6] Carl von Kraus, *Des Minnesangs Frühling,* Untersuchungen (Leipzig, 1939), p. 436.

[7] Set to music twice by Heinrich Isaac (*ca.* 1450–1517):
a. before 1500, probably as a canonical tenor song.
b. famous homophonic version with *cantus firmus* in the upper voice (discant song) = No. 36 in Georg Forster I, ¹1539, ⁵1560 (*Erbe deutscher* Musik, vol. 20 [1942]), reprint also in *Denkmäler der Tonkunst in Oesterreich,* vol. XIV, pt. 1.

Minnesang studies, the sequence of words has been paid scant attention, but a few examples from Walther von der Vogelweide alone turn
them up, too, within the frame of reference of the "going abroad"
motif (44,15) : "ist daz ein minne dandern suochen sol,/so wirt sie vil
dicke ellende/mit gedanken als ich bin." Here "sie" refers to the lady
in the distance (compare also Walther 13,5, and for the words versus
works formula, Walther 14,6/7).

Within the scope of the minstrel-crusader performance it appears
clear that "ellenden" means to undertake the dangerous campaign to
the Holy Land. Thus the very next line can underscore: "Nu seht"—
by the sign of the cross, perhaps along with a gesture—how it—that is,
the love of God—"mich uz miner zunge" (draws me from my home,
my language, my song) draws me across the sea (*ziuhet uber mer*).
The refinement and the main *pointe* of the poem consist, however, in
the fact that this obligation, which is without question and is visible in
the sign of the cross, is imposed by the text of the song upon the
"Frauenminne-Diener" (servants of love for a mortal lady).

What does this "ellenden" mean, which is required of them as a
"work," this "ellenden" in which obviously the obligation of the one
kind of *minne* finds its peak. Certainly it means *minne* from afar,
"Fern-Minne" in every literal and transferred sense of *Minnesang* and
its *minne* dialectic from von Hausen until the late thirteenth century,
that is, "hohe Minne" in general. (There are parallels to the service
symbol of the cross in the symbols of service to the lady in the epic such
as sleeves, veils, and mirrors.) For it would suggest itself once more
that Hartmann here, just as in the case of the *Minne* captivity, is appeal-
ing more to the frame of reference provided by the epic than that of the
song, which would plead also for the unified view of service *minne* of
the song and the marriage *minne* of the epic simply as "hohe Minne."
But no deeds follow upon this earthly *minne* from afar; how could they,
and where would they be directed, since their whole dialectical basis in
the minnesong exists only as a reflection that has no expectation of
success and a sublimated boasting about them?

The act of distant love on the part of the singer, and here on the
part of Hartmann, is literally the journey into exile, to the Holy Land.
This must be the message heightened by the last two lines of the

strophe, 218,19/20, in order finally to bring them to bear. They can and must mean only: nothing but my captivity to love, the love of God, could bring me out of my own land into exile. The death of his master, which is mourned in a very moving fashion in other poems (*MF* 206,14; 210,23 ff.) (that is the conjecture of Hermann Paul, which was taken up into the text by Carl von Kraus), has no justification here and would in fact be deprived of its justification. But even the death of "her Saladin" and all of his army, which the manuscript provides and many of the interpreters accept, is quite irrelevant for the dialectics of this poem. I take up a conjecture of Günther Jungbluth (*Euphorion* 49 [1955] pp 144–162) with a slight variation, which removes this crux in a radical manner and as I believe completely in the sense of the song and I read: "und lieze si [that is, Minne] mich, her Saladin und al sin her die enbræhten mich von Vranken niemer einen fuoz"—that is: and if she, that Mistress *Minne* (the crusade *minne* which compels me as her captive to keep the pledge I offered, upon having been granted quarter) would leave me free, if she were to release me from this promise of mutual obligation (see below), then Sir Saladin and all his army (that is, all those completely or at least partially terrestrial or chivalric motivations) could not bring me one foot out of Franconia (for this specification of place, see Jungbluth)! Saladin is still alive for me, then, and the crusade is that of 1189, but any further biographical exploitation of the poem has become highly questionable in view of the new artistic aspect of the role of the minstrel. (I can also therefore no longer believe in the role of Barbarossa which is suggested by Jungbluth.)

What the second strophe provides is in a much more decisive manner the definition of *minne,* which Hartmann steadfastly presents as one and the same, independent of the figure of the partner, whether it be God and Christ or the lady of terrestrial *minne.* What is common in both and identical is for him the obligation to service. But that is completely unconditional. Mere reflection about it, which suffices for all minnesongs, does not suffice for him. He criticizes it in the very next (third) strophe as false expectation (*wan*). What he demands and merely demonstrates in the crusader's role are deeds, thus in most general terms, "*minne* from afar," which is performed and not merely reflected upon. This is a radically religious and at the same time internal criticism of *Minnesang*. It proves to us that in the conventional agreement of the members of the profession, and in the public mind as well, the earthly love of a lady did not mean simply the experience of love but included, as its living base, a moral claim upon the total personality, which must "sich ellenden," lose itself in order to gain itself. With that, broad perspectives into the world of the medieval mind, of the courtly lay literature, are opened. I cannot and will not go further into that, but refer to my earlier attempts in this direction, particularly with respect to Hartmann's epics.[8] From this position, that is, the definition of the one *minne,* as *minne* from afar, as "hohe Minne," and the criticism of its false servants, Hartmann attacks the members of the guild themselves in the third strophe and addresses them directly: "Ir minnesinger. . . ." That which falsifies their song is *der wan* (false expectation). This difficult concept when seen from the vantage point of the second strophe must here signify the inactive reflections of *Minnesang*. However, the criticism is provided with a new basis. Continuing to be purposely rough in his tone, Hartmann offers a "proper" song for one and the same love still inexplicitly present in a visible form only in the sign of the cross: "Ich wil mich rüemen, ich mac wol von minne singen" (218,23) (I make the boast about myself that I know how to sing about *minne*). The distinguishing difference is, however, now formed by the goal of the service, the mutuality of the love: "sit mich diu minne [love viewed abstractly and the beloved concretely] hat und ich si han. Daz ich da wil, seht[in the sign of the cross] das wil also gerne haben mich. So müezt ab ir verliezen under wilen wanes vil: ir ringent umbe liep daz iuwer niht enwil" (since love has me and I have her. That which I desire, see [by the sign of the cross] that desires me equally. Thus you must often lose the object of your expectation: you struggle for love which wants none of you).

---

[8] H. Kuhn, *"Erec," Festschrift für P. Kluckhohn und H. Schneider* (Tübingen, 1948), pp. 122–147; now also in Kuhn, *Dichtung und Welt im Mittelalter* (Stuttgart 1959), pp. 133–150. See also C. Cormeau, *Hartmanns von Aue "Armer Heinrich" und "Gregorius." Studien zur Interpretation mit dem Blick auf die Theologie zur Zeit Hartmanns* (Munich, 1966) (Münchener Texte und Untersuchungen zur deutschen Literatur des Mittelalters 15).

What is the nature of the problem of mutual love in the minnesong from the earliest period up to Walther and then Neidhart and onward? This has always been viewed as an experiential problem, which amounts to: does he get her or not? Hartmann provides us with a more precise key. In strophe II he had given the definition: courtly is "love from afar"; it means "exile." Its significance is not to be found in the ambience of the *grande passion,* where the one and only beloved determines life and fate by whether "boy gets girl" or not, and determines whether the lover's fate is to be a happy one or, as is the rule in fiction through *Anna Karenina,* a tragic one. Courtly love is, or should always be, mutual love. Its goal is always union with the beloved, but union in its absolute sense as the highest earthly "salvation," as the *summum bonum* on earth, even as something intended by God. And that is the way, the only way, all the poets of courtly love sing it.

But in our poem, Hartmann opposes to the rhetorical "love from afar" of his trade the literal "love from afar" of religion, and he does so with exquisite literalness. They woo a "love that wants them not." As far as the poet is concerned, they are wrecked by their earthly partner in love, the lady, because her distance is realizable only in a social sense and excludes any transcendental response to their love. But Christ is the partner in a "love from afar" which on the one hand one never really "has," except perhaps after death, but which even "loved us first" (see page 35). Hartmann has apparently despaired and thus been wrecked on the earthly "salvation" of love, the ethical qualification of the knight by earthly "love from afar" which the *minne* poets incessantly reflect. This is not surprising if one considers his *minne* poetry and his romances with all their love-guilt problems which distinguish him from the other poets. But it also proves to us that here he, too, obviously counting on the understanding of the public and of his colleagues, is able to ascribe to all of minnesong, or at least to the German branch of it, a goal that not only far exceeds the usual mere casuistry of love and also the category of the so-called courtly virtues but even demands union with the beloved partner, indeed must demand it, as the greatest good, *summum bonum,* lady or Christ. And that is the way the closing line summarizes it: "Why can't you poor fellows love as I do?" "To love such a love" (*minnen solhe minne*) permits the love partner an indeterminacy between personified abstraction and tender address to child, man, woman, Christ, God. The "poorness" of the love servants of a courtly lady does not stem simply from the fact that the beloved does not listen to their plea. They are poor because all their suffering of "love from afar" does not suffice to force an answer from the highest partner, because, in short, they can not love high enough for a union with the transcendently real being of the partner.

alliteration and sound repetition in the lyrics of oswald von wolkenstein

BY   W.   T.   H.   J A C K S O N

In reading the lyrics of Oswald von Wolkenstein, I was struck by the amount of assonance and alliteration to be found in his poetry. Such devices are not at all common in the earlier *Minnesang,* and it seemed that the poet was perhaps using these sound repetitions as part of a deliberate pattern and not merely to reinforce his meaning. Further examination showed that there were occasions on which the poet piled up alliteration and assonance in sheer exuberance, while in other instances their occurrence seemed part of a pattern extending through a whole poem. In these latter cases, the technique was often subtle, involving slight, progressive sound changes from the first word of a series through those that follow. It may be noted in this connection that it is often impossible to preserve the formal distinction between rhyme and assonance in discussing these sound patterns, since a pattern that seems like internal rhyme in one strophe may prove, by comparison with the corresponding part of the other strophes, to be an intensified assonance pattern. As we examine the various sound patterns, we should bear in mind that the spelling of words is by no means an infallible guide to sound correspondence. We would expect that in Oswald's dialect *p* would alliterate with *b*, *g* with *k*, and *t* with *d*, but it should also be noted that he rhymes the vowel sounds *ei, ai, ie,* and even *i.* We shall now examine some of the poems with a view to determining the alliterative techniques used and attempt to draw some conclusions.

Examples of simple alliteration are widespread, and there is no necessity to give more than a few examples. Let us look at the text of poem number 11 in Karl Kurt Klein's edition (except s for long es) of the works.*

* All quotations in this article are from *Die Lieder Oswalds von Wolkenstein,* ed. Karl Kurt Klein (Tübingen: Niemeyer, 1962). Of the numerous articles written about Oswald, none, to my knowledge, has any direct bearing on the subject of this paper, but reference may be made to the following biblio-

I   O snöde werlt,
                     wie lang ich leib und güt in dir vorslisse,
                     so vind ich dich neur itel swach
                     mit wort, werk und gepërde;
                     der untreu bistu also vol,
                     das ich das ort noch end begreiffen kan.
                     Falsch bösen gelt
                     fürstu luglich, truglichen gar zu flisse.
                     mit mü und arbait, ungemach
                     und groblichem gevërde,
                     so ringstu nach der helle hal.
                     das klagt, ir tummen frauen und ouch man.
                     Tëglichen stick wir tag und nacht
                     nach güt und werltlich er,
                     wirt unser will dar inn volbracht,
                     so hab wir doch nicht mer,
                     neur klaine speis und swachs gewand,
                     und was wir güts bi dem han fürgesant.

II   Vil mancher spricht,
                     in rechter treu sol ich in allzeit vinden
                     mit leib und güt zu meim gebot
                     vest ewiklichen stëte.
                     köm ich mit armüt in sein haus,
                     er wolt, ich wër ain fuxs in ainem hag.
                     Klain zuversicht
                     wir haben söllen zu des Adams kindern,

---

graphical material: Friedrich Neumann, "Oswald von Wolkenstein," in: Wolfgang Stammler, *Die Deutsche Literatur des Mittelalters, Verfasserlexikon* 5
(1955), 814–830; Karl Kurt Klein, "Oswald von Wolkenstein, ein Dichter,
ein Komponist und Sänger des Spätmittelalters: Forschungsergebnisse und
Aufgaben," *Wirkendes Wort,* 13 (1963), 1–12. I have made a great deal of
use of the excellent study of Oswald's language by Friedrich Maurer, *Beiträge
zur Sprache Oswalds von Wolkenstein,* Giessener Beiträge, III (1922). The
recent article by Christoph Petzsch, "Meistersinger Reime in Mozartbriefen,"
Euphorion, 60 (1966), 273–276, seems to lend some support to the idea that
the use of specific words and word combinations could be relied upon to produce
an effect in the areas of the southern-German-speaking area in which the
Meistersang was widespread.

neur dienen aim, der haisset got;
die werlt fürt ungeräte.
darab so nim dir ainen graus
und hoff zu dem, der dir gehelfen mag.
Ach, mir erbarmt manger güter man
und ich mir selber ouch,
der da nit recht bedenken kan,
wie gar es ist ain rouch
der werlde dienst mit grosser not.
was ist der lon, wenn man spricht, er ist tod?

III   Kain ermer vich
under allen tieren kund ich nie ervaren,
neur aines haisst ein hofeman,
der geit sich gar für aigen
dem herren sein umb klainen sold.
des tët ain esel nicht, und wer er frei.
Reit, slach und stich,
zuck, raub und brenn, den menschen tü nicht sparen,
nim ross und wagen, henn und han,
gen niemant tü dich naigen;
gedenk, dein herr der werd dir hold,
wenn er von dir sicht sölche stampanei.
Du ste vor im, tritt hinden nach
und kapf den langen tag,
ist er ain fürst, für in so gach,
das er dich sehen mag:
sprech er zu dir ain freuntlich wort,
das nemst du für des himel fürsten hort.

IV   Ir vogelein
und andre tier, baide wilde und die zamen,
ir traget rechte liebe gar;
geleich kiest sein geleichen,
gemahel sein gemähelein
in nöten si bei ainander bleiben stän.
Die freunde mein,
solt ich vor in erkrumben und erlamen,
e das mir ainer gäb sein nar

und solt mich do mit reichen
zu meim gesunt an mailes pein,
ich müsst vor im ee als der sne zergän.
Des menschen lieb wer gar enwicht,
die ains dem andern tüt,
hett wir der gab nit zuversicht
und hoffnung umb das güt.
mein aigen kind gewun vordriess,
wesst es die leng von mir nicht seinen geniess.

V   Und solt ich mir
erwünschen gar nach meines herzen freude
ain leben selber, wie ich wolt,
mit hilf aller maister sinne,
so künd ichs doch bedenken nicht,
oder ich müsst die leng vordriessen darinn han.
Was hilft mein gier
zu grossem güt und nach der eren geude?
was hilft mich silber oder gold?
was hilft der frauen minne,
seid wertlich freud pald ist enwicht,
und wais gar wol, das ich schier müss darvon?
Turnier und stich, louff, tanz und spring
auf ainem weiten platz,
mach kurzweil vil, treib hoflich ding,
verdrä dich als ain katz,
und wenn der schimpf all da ergat,
gee wider dar, so vindst ain öde stat.

VI   Ach freunt, gesell,
du zweifel nicht, was ich dir hie wil sagen,
dien got von ganzem herzen dein,
lass dir die werlt nicht smecken,
aus irem lust mach dir ain spot,
so hastu freude hie und dort genüg.
Kain ungevell
las dich bekümern, das dich mach verzagen,
kain trübsail las dir pringen pein.
ob leiden dich wil wecken,

das ist ain sunder gnad von got,
dieselbig gnad zuckt dir der helle lüg.
Wer sich den zoren binden lat,
der gleicht sich ainem vich,
und dem got hie verlihen hat
fünf sinn vernünftiklich;
das ist die höchste wirdikait,
wer weislich vicht in widerwertikait.

VII   Mich wundert ser,
das wir auf diser werlt so vil entpauen
und sehen wol, wie es ergät.
wo sind mein freund, gesellen?
wo sein mein eldern, vodern hin?
so sein wir all neur uber hundert jar?
Mich wundert mer,
das ich mich nie kund mässen meiner frauen,
die mich so lang betrogen hat
mit grossem ungevellen.
mich hat geplennt mein tummer sin
und nie bekant, das si mir was gevar.
Wir pauen hoch auf ainen tant
an heusern, vesten, zier,
und tät doch gar ain slechte wand,
die lenger werdt dann wir.
volg, brüder, swester, arm und reich,
pau dort ain sloss, das dich werdt ewikleich.

The first strophe contains a wealth of words that alliterate with *w*.
Each of the first four lines contains at least one example. But the alliteration is not merely a sound effect, which would in any case be
pointless here. The alliteration links *werlt*, *wort*, and *werk*, a significant triad in a poem whose opening line is "O snöde werlt." Here there
appears to be a logical purpose for the alliteration, but what shall we
say of lines 7 and 8? The alliteration of *f* and of *l* is very obvious. So is
the assonantal play *luglich/truglich*. The words are associated in meaning and are clearly reinforcing one another in sound and significance.
A look at the other strophes reveals no corresponding pattern, unless

the two verbs beginning with *er* in strophe IV are to be so construed, so that there is no pattern, but merely reinforcing alliteration.

Oswald is fond of such repetitive sounds—"groblichem gevërde," "helle hal," "teglichen . . . tag," "slach und stich," "henn und han," "herr . . . hold." Many of these are popular pairs, words habitually joined in popular speech, and Oswald uses them to make his points perhaps more instinctively than consciously. Their use makes it clear, if confirmation were needed, that Oswald's language is deeply rooted in popular speech, but it reveals little about the structure of his lyrics. In the same poem there are examples of more deliberate alliteration. In strophe V Oswald launches into a complicated alliterative series—*gier, güt, geude, gold*—which is clearly a grouping of the pleasures of the world, and follows it with a series of *f/v* alliterations—*frauen, freud, wertlich, enwicht, wars, wol*—which emphasizes the same pattern. It is not hard to find other poems in which this intensification by alliteration occurs. In number 50, for example, alliteration and assonance are used to intensify the spring description:

mai   mit   lieber
erd   bedecket
eben   berg
erklingen   singen   hohen   hal
gauch   fleuch   hinden   hin
vogel   gogel
hunger   lunger
ellend   wellent
ich   vich

The alliteration in this poem reaches its peak with whole lines representing birdcalls. This type of alliteration can scarcely be called patterned. Nor is it new in Middle High German poetry. It is dependent on the subject matter and is the most natural use of alliteration: to reinforce by sound the meaning of a passage.

It is often hard to determine when alliteration becomes internal rhyme. If we examine poem number 21, an exuberant comic piece full of alliterative effects, we are immediately struck by the frequent occurrence of apparent internal rhyme:

	I	II	III
	I	II	III
1	weib freut		
3	meie geschraie	gug gugk ruck	phlicht angesicht
4	krafft safft	vil saitenspil	mait trait
5		baissen biersen schiessen	
7	wecken recken	mait beklait	wenglin hendlin
8	plüd müd	breis hofeweis	leut gedreut
9		gezellt gevellt	mich machen krank
10			gewunden krump
11	verneut eur		
12	welgt gel		
13	freulin gailt		
14	gepawer reut		

It will be observed that only in lines 3, 4, and 8 can we speak of true internal rhyme, if we assume that such rhyme is a regular feature of the strophic pattern, that it occurs in the same position, and that full rhyme is involved. Yet *weib* and *freut* are almost certainly in assonance, and in line 7 of the first two strophes there is full rhyme between two adjacent words. Only in the third is there assonance that is very close to rhyme between two words, the second of which is removed from the first. Clearly these sound connections are no more part of the rhyming patterns than the *welgt/gel* of I,12, and the *baissen/biersen, schiessen* of II,5, but equally clearly Oswald intends them to have a pleasurable aesthetic effect akin to that of rhyme. This is particularly true of II,5, where Oswald is making use of the technique of progressive assonance discussed later. The alliteration reflects meaning in the sense that the activity, hunting, is given its intensity by repeated words of associated meaning which vary by one syllable only and retain the sibilant throughout. More often, however, Oswald seems to write a line with simple alliteration without particular regard to meaning. Such an apparently irrational technique stems from his method of amplification. No attempt is made to enlarge the narrative content of a strophe, but a number of graphic words, usually nouns or infinitives of verbs, are added to intensify the reader's verbal and musical impressions. The rhetorical figure is, of course, *frequentatio*, but its use is often little more than an excuse for alliterative effect, with the meaning secondary to the sound. In the poem we have just mentioned, we may note *klumpern/klingen, zünglin/zangen, snüren/unden, frünt/schuch*, and many others. Almost any of the poems which are not of a serious moral or religious nature (and some of those which are) will provide examples of this technique, which is, of course, closely associated with the use of very short lines, often consisting of only two words with rhyme.

A special type of alliteration which may be mentioned is that which occurs in column, that is, in successive lines rather than in the same line. Frequently such column alliteration is part of an elaborately wrought pattern of rhyme and alliteration and will be discussed under that head, but sometimes its use appears to have the object of linking strophes. In poem number 34, for example, we find that in line 5 of each of the three strophes there are words ending in *lich*. There is no question of a rhyme scheme here, since the words appear irregularly and the lines already have an elaborate internal rhyme scheme of their own (*jan/ kan/verstan, bricht/ticht/flicht, erlöst/tröst/höchst*). Not counting the rhymes in the second strophe, there are six words in *ich* in the three fifth lines, surely no accident. Lines 1 and 3 in each strophe show similar vertical assonance—*vein/rain, gogeleichen/vogelreich, feuer/ abenteuer*. If we assume that in Oswald's dialect *eu* was pronounced like *ai*, there is assonance throughout. Poem 35 probably exhibits the same technique: *braiten/freut, got/rot, esel/sesel*. It is poem number 43, however, which shows the technique at its best. In the seventh and ninth lines of each strophe there appear two words that rhyme or come close to rhyming—*verellendt/wellend, kaines/klaines, weiplich/ leiplich, weis/leiser, übet/betrübet, schendet/verphendet, bedarf/ scharpf*—but whose varying positions in the line seem to preclude their being part of a strict rhyming pattern. There are similar echoing sounds in lines 3 and 6 in most but not all of the strophes: *tugentlichen/ unterteniklich, triegen/klüger, klüg/betrubt, tüt/übels, gert/wer*. But these are unimportant compared with the proliferation of alliterating sounds in strophe VI—*smäh/sicherlichen/schaden/schendet/schulde* —which is clearly intended to intensify the emotional pleading by the man in this *pastourelle*-type poem and also, perhaps, gives us a hint of what he really intends. Oswald is particularly fond of vertical sound repetition in his numerous refrains. In poem number 83, for example,

we find *rotter/rain, versüsst/füsslin, baine/brüstlin, geferte/verget.*
The refrains offer many more instances of the same technique.

A most interesting variant of the vertical alliteration technique is to be found in poem number 70.

I   Her wiert, uns dürstet also sere,
        trag auf wein! trag auf wein! trag auf wein!
        Das dir got dein laid verkere,
        pring her wein! pring her wein! pring her wein!
        Und dir dein sälden mere,
        nu schenck ein! nu schenck ein! nu schenck ein!

II   Gretel, wiltu sein mein treutel?
        so sprich, sprichs! so sprichs! so sprich, sprichs!
        Ja koufst du mir ainen beutel,
        leicht tün ichs, leicht tün ichs, leicht tün ichs,
        Und reiss mir nit das heutel,
        neur stich, stichs! neur stich, stichs! neur stich, stichs!

III   Sim Jensel, wiltus mit mir tanzen?
        so kom auch! so kom auch! so kom auch!
        Böckisch well wir umbhin ranzen,
        Jans, nit strauch! Jans, nit strauch! Jans, nit strauch!
        Und schon mir meiner schranzen,
        dauch schon, dauch! dauch nach, dauch! dauch, Jensel, dauch!

IV   Pfeiff auff, Hainzel, Lippel, snäggel!
        frisch, frow, fri! frisch, frow, fri! frisch, frow, fri!
        Zwait eu, rürt eu, snurra, bäggel!
        Jans, Lutzei, Cünz, Kathrei, Benz, Clarei,
        spring kelbrisch, durta Jäckel!
        ju haig, haig! ju, haig haig! ju, haig, haig!

V   Hin get der raie, seusa, möstel!
        nu reckt an! nu reckt an! nu reckt an!
        gump auf, Hainreich, noch ain jösstel;
        rür, biderbman! rür, biderbman! rür, biderbman! rür, biderbman!
        Metz Diemut, deut das kösstel!
        dran, dran, dran! dran, dran, dran! dran, dran, dran!

VI   Nu füdert eu, man isst im dorfe,
       nempt kain weil! nempt kain weil! nempt kain weil!
       nachin, Cünrat, fauler thschorfe,
       du lempeil! du lempeil! du lempeil!
       lüg umb dich als ain orfe,
       eil, held, eil! eil, held, eil! eil, eil, eil!

The even lines are a type of refrain, usually a command three times repeated. One syllable in each line is repeated vertically, *ein* in the first strophe, *ichs* in the second, *auch* in the third, *ei* in the fourth, *an* in the fifth, and *eil* in the sixth. The sounds taken together constitute a primitive call to action which is in complete consonance with the spirit of the poem.

Oswald's use of what is here called progressive assonance and alliteration is frequent and clearly intentional, but it is not easy to see what effects were intended. Let us examine a few examples—for instance, the first few lines of poem number 83. *Jetterin junck* is a normal enough alliteration, but *frisch* changes one sound to *frei* and then follows the further change to *früt,* a gradation of sounds and incidentally a combination that Oswald uses more than once. It is not hard to find other examples—*Keuschlich geboren/ain kind so küne* and *veind/sein/schricklich/ser/erloschen* from poem number 38 and *krispel/krumpel, krinnen/krauss, edel/adeleicher/schein* from poem number 61. These and most other examples seem to be spontaneous sound combinations of the ding, dang, dong variety which are common in popular poetry and appropriate to Oswald, but occasionally he uses them in a pattern. Poem number 68 offers some good examples.

I   Mein herz jüngt sich in hoher gail
      und ist getrösst, erlösst von lieber hand,
      Die mir zu fleiss frei tadels mail
      zärtlich erschoss, entsloss all meine band
      so gar an strëfflich schand.
      Ich lob den tag, stund, weil, die zeit, minut und quint,
      do ich es hort und gaistlich sach,
      Das mir mein klag unzweifelichen so geswind
      ward abgenomen; do zerbrach
      meins herzen ungemach.

II   Mit eren, o ausserweltes G,
so freust du mich glich inn der sele grund;
Darnach ain edel R und E
mich trösten sol so wol durch rotten mund,
frölich zu aller stund.
An end der wort zwai T beslossen han die treu
von dir zu mir in ewikait.
Mein höchster hort, das lass dir teglich wesen neu,
und desgeleichen ich berait
mit ganzer stetikait.

III   Vergiss durch all dein weiplich er,
wo ich dein zucht, frucht je erzürnet han.
Für all diss werlt liept mir dein er
und wil der vil bas wesen undertan,
löblich an abelan.
Ungeschaiden hie auff erd bis in den tod,
und darnach hundert tausend jar.
Von uns baiden kain falsche zung das bettenbrot
sol freuen mer, klain umb ain här;
herz lieb, got füg das wär!

In the middle of the second line of each strophe there are two words that rhyme. The same is true of the fourth lines, except that in the third strophe the words are *wil* and *vil,* and they do not occupy the usual position in the line. It seems to me that we are less concerned with rhyme in the formal sense than with patterned alliteration, for there is considerable variation of the sound pattern in all those already mentioned, and similar patterns occur in other lines but not in all strophes:

I   getrösst/erlösst, fleiss/frei/mail, erschoss/entsloss,
strefflich/schand
II   mich/glich/inn, sol/so/wol, höchster/hort
III   zucht/frucht, wil/vil, mer/här

Oswald does not hesitate to establish an apparent pattern in two or more strophes and then abandon it in others, as we shall see.

There are poems of which large parts seem to have been written mainly to see what alliterative effects could be produced and where the effect is an end in itself. Poem number 82 is an excellent example. Although the verses have some interesting features, I shall quote here only the refrain:

> Frisch, frei, fro, frölich,
> ju, jutz, jölich,
> gail, gol, gölich, gogeleichen,
> hurtig, tum, tümbrisch,
> knawss, bumm, bümbrisch,
> tentsch, krumb, rümblisch, rogeleichen,
> so ist mein herz an allen smerz,
> wenn ich an sich meins lieben bülen gleichen.

Here we have sheer alliterative exuberance. All the lines except the last two show the alliterative progression of which we have already spoken, although the method varies. In the first three lines the initial sound is retained throughout, and the vowels are changed. In the fourth line the vowel is retained and the consonants changed, while in the fifth and sixth both types are combined. The pattern is made yet more complex by the fact that the last words of the first and second lines rhyme with the penultimate word of the third line, and the same is done in lines 4, 5, and 6, with the additional rhyming of the middle words of lines 4 and 5. The last words of the third and sixth lines, the only four-syllable words in the refrain, also rhyme, indeed correspond exactly except for the first sound, and both rhyme with the last word of the refrain. Now even Oswald's best friend would hardly argue that the refrain makes much sense, but as a sound pattern it is extremely complex and shows the author's delight in combining the ridiculous with the artful.

A similar and even more complicated technique is to be observed in poem number 92.

> "Treib her, treib überher, du trautes Berbelin das mein,
> zu mir ruck mit den schäfflin dein,
> kom schier, mein schönes Berbelin!"
> "Ich merck, ich merck dich wol, aber ich entün sein wërlich nicht,
> dein waide, die ist gar enwicht,
> mein haide stat in grüne phlicht."

"Mein waid, mein waid, die ist wol auss der massen kurlich güt,
mit kle, loub, gras vil plümlin plüt,
der snee get ab in meiner hüt."
"So hör, so hör ich hie vil süsser vogelin gesangk,
da bei ist mir die weil nicht lanck,
gar frei ist aller mein gedanckh."
"So han, so han ich hie wol ain külen, klaren brunn,
dorumb ain schatten für die sunn.
nu kum, meins herzen höchste wunn!"
"Von durst, von durst so hab ich kainerlaie hendlin not,
ja keut ich nie das käss und brot
von heut, das mir mein mütter bot."
"Vil swammen, swemmelein, die wachsen hie in diesem strauch
darzu vil junger voglin rauch.
kämstu zu mir, ich gäb dir ouch."
"Wiltu, wiltu mich sichern, genzlichen mit gemache län,
villeicht so treib ich zu dir hnan;
susst weicht mein vich verrlich herdan."
"Nu fürcht, nu fürcht dich nicht, mein ausserwelte schöne tock!
ja flicht ich dir deinen weissen lock."
und slicht dir deinen rotten rock."
"Das hastu, das hastu mir so dick versprochen bei der wid,
vest stet zu halden ainen frid,
noch tet du mir an meim gelid."
"Der schad, der schad was klaine, der deinem leib allda beschach,
in mass, als es dein swester sprach;
ich lass dich fürbass mit gemach."
"Das wirt, das wirt sich sagen erst, so ich werden sol ain braut,
ob sich verraucket hat mein haut.
pfüg dich, du tet mirs gar zu laut."
"Bis wil, bis wilkomen, du wunniklicher, schöner hort!
du bist mir lieber hie wann dort.
nu lisp mir zu ain freuntlich wort!"
"Und wer, und wer ich dort, wer wer dann, lieb bei dir allhie?
mein herz dich genzlich nie verlie
an smerz, du waisst wol selber, wie."
"Des wol, des wol, mich ward vilmer wann hundert tausend stund.
mich trösst dein röselochter mund,
der lösst auf sweres herzen punt."

Vil freud, vil freud und wunne, ir baider leib all do betrat,
bis raid der aubent zuher jat.
an laid schied sich ir baider wat.

The most obvious feature is the repeated phrase at the beginning of the third line of each strophe, not a surprising occurrence in a dialogue poem. We are also accustomed by now to lines that play on variations on sound patterns, such as "keut ich nie käss," "weicht mein vich verrlich," "lass fürbass mit gemach," and "bis wil, bis wilkommen." Such lines are the normal stuff of Oswald's poetry. More interesting, because it is clearly a *tour de force*, is the vertical assonance of the poem. Bear in mind that Oswald often uses the sounds *i, ie, ei,* and *ai* in rhyming positions, and then observe the beginnings of his lines. The pattern is one of uninterrupted assonance of these sounds. The second and third line of each triplet rhymes its second word or sound (*mir/schier, waide/ haide, kle/sne, dorumb/nu kumb,* and so on, and these rhyming sounds very frequently show some correspondence with the sounds of the first part of each first line. The second and third lines are connected in another way, by consonant alliteration of words in their middle part— for example, *schäfflin/schönes* in lines 2 and 3, *gar/grüner* in lines 5 and 6, and *gras/get* in lines 8 and 9. It is clear that here, as so often, the poet is using patterned alliteration for its own sake, without reference to the meaning of the poem. The sound pattern is an end in itself.

An equally fascinating assonantal picture appears in poem number 93.

Ia   ... prich! rich! sich:
                            scherz dringt,
                            zwingt und pringt
                            natürlich lieb in immer.
                            ach, rach, grimmiklichen schrei.
                            ei frei, gesell,
                            kenn dein treu be ...

Ib   Herz, prich! sich; smerz
                            hie ser und pringt
                            natürlich lib
                            ich immer, ach, rach

ich grimmiklichen schrei.
frei, gesell,
wenn dein treu bedencken.

II   Hort mein, dein ain
wort mort mir gail.
unhail das sail
ich schreiben tün an wage schild.
wild mild mein herz begriffen hat,
quat mat. nu snell,
gelück, rück mir lieb verrencken!

III   Tod, laid, maid, schaid
not! rot dein mund
trost wund die hund,
der stimm mir nie wolt louffen süss.
büss müss mir freuden werden an,
wan man, gesell,
nie lie plausen auff schrenken

Since the text of strophe I appears to be imperfect, I shall refer to it only occasionally in the following analysis. Here is the sound pattern of the poem reduced to its basic form:

```
er    ich   ich   er
ie    er    i
i     i
ich   i     ach   ach
ich   i     i     ich   ei
ei          ell
e     ei    eu    encken


or    ei    ei    ai
or    or    i     ei
ai    ai
i     ei    ü     a     ild
ild   ild   ei    er    i     at
at    at    u     ell
ück   ück   i     ie    encken
```

```
o    ai   ai   ai
o    o    ei   und
o    und  i    und
i    i    ie   o    ou   üss
üss  üss  i    eu   er   an
an   an   ell
ie   ie   au   au   encken
```

Clearly assonance is intended between the two adjacent words in the middle of the first line of each strophe. In two of the three it extends to three words, a fact that raises doubts about the reading in strophe Ia. The vowel of the first word in line 1 invariably assonances with the second vowel of line 2 and, except in Ia, with the first word of the second line also. This triangle pattern is found also in lines 4 and 5, 6 and 7 in the last two strophes (*schild/wild/mild, süss/büss/müss, hat/ quat/mat, an/wan/man*). Lines 2 and 3 show a slight variation—assonance of the last word of line 2 with the second and last syllables of line 3. These sound relations are, of course, rhymes, but in the corresponding positions in the first strophe we find *ach/rach/ich* and *schrei/frei/ gesell*. (The defective first strophe has, more reasonably, *schrei/ei/ frei*.) The probability is that in positions like these Oswald regarded an alliteration like *ich/ach* as sufficient for his pattern. This impression is confirmed by the group *pringt/natürlich/lib* of Ia. Finally let us note the pattern in the last line of the last two strophes, where the first two words rhyme and the second two are in assonance. In the whole poem the "*ei* rhyme group" vowels occur forty-two times out of a total of eighty-six in the vowels shown in the above pattern (some unstressed vowels have been omitted). If we include the possible assonances with *eu* and *ü*, the total rises to forty-eight. I need hardly say that this is a difficult poem to interpret, and fortunately this is no part of my task, but it is worth noting that the assonance and rhyme within the lines is frequently designed to give an effect of oxymoron by attracting attention to the opposed meanings of the like-sounding words.

There are numerous poems where Oswald seems to start a pattern and fails to carry it through. Let us examine poem number 103.

I   Wer die ougen will verschüren mit den brenden,
             sein leben enden, mit güten zenden

übel essen, ligen in dem stro,
der füg sich in die Lumpardie,
da vil manger wirt unfro.
tieff ist das kot, teuer das brot,
ungötlich reu mit falscher treu
sol man da vinden tëglichen neu.
das ist ain speis, der ich nicht keu.

II   Wer nach der wage ringe hechten kouffen welle,
für ungevelle so fail, geselle,
ainen, der ain staine leber trag:
forsch in des kaisers canzelie,
wo man solche fisch erjag.
Gülcher, mach kund, was galt ain pfund?
pro zingk soldin et tre zesin,
also galt sich das leberlin vin
von disem sütten hechtigin.

III   Herman, Marquart, Costnitz, Ulmen wër das leben
uns freud zu geben von mündlin eben,
und mein öheim hinder dem ofen wër,
das wër ain besser stampanie,
wan das uns der peutel ler
wirt zu Placenz. mein conscienz
wirt offt so swach, wie wol ich lach,
so das mein schreiber, dick gefach,
klagt seinen grossen ungemach.

IV   Sebastian, wërst dus ain oxs zu Florenzöla
oder ain caniöla und zugst cum döla
tëglich misst auff ainem wagen gross,
das nëm ich für ain süssen breie.
für wär, ich geb dir auch ain stoss
zu deiner brust, als du mir tüst
mit valscher gier, grob als ain stier;
zwar desgeleichen videlt ich dir,
und wurd dir mer, das stünd zü mir.

In the first strophe we have a clear rhyme pattern: *brenden/enden/
zenden* in lines 1 and 2, *kot/brot* in line 6, and *reu/treu/neu/keu* in
lines 7, 8, and 9, This rhyme pattern is repeated in all strophes and

follows the triangle form of which Oswald is fond. But in the first two strophes there is a distinct alliterative pattern (*wer/wil* and *wer/wage*) which is not repeated in the last two strophes. *Leben ende* and *ungevelle fail* in the second lines of these strophes may be accidental, but this can hardly be so in the sixth lines of strophes I, II, and IV, in which alliteration occurs (*tieff/teuer, Gülcher/kund/galt, deiner/du/tust*). Yet strophe III shows not the slightest sign of alliteration. On the other hand, in the seventh line we find *zingk/zesin, wirt/wie/wol,* and *gier/grob* in the last three strophes, but nothing that corresponds in the first. This kind of thing occurs so often that the conclusion is inescapable that Oswald would use what we may call a supplemental pattern of alliteration if it fitted in easily with his meaning but would not go to any trouble to make it consistent. In other words, there would be a fixed pattern of rhyme, often with internal rhyme and sometimes alliteration and assonance, and a more flexible pattern of alliteration which need not be carried through in every strophe.

It is now time to examine some of the more complicated patterns that Oswald uses, and again it should be pointed out that the distinction between rhyme and assonance is often blurred. We can legitimately speak of end rhyme and internal rhyme when the rhyming words occur in a fixed position in the interior of a line. But when the position is not fixed and especially when, in short lines, almost every word rhymes with something, it is perhaps more just to speak of a pattern of assonance. I shall try to give examples of those patterns that Oswald seems to favor and make some comments on them.

Poem number 78 is a relatively simple affair:

I   Mich tröst ain adeliche mait,
          die ist für war durch klar an tadels mail.
          Der keuschlich er ist wol so brait,
          das si verdeckt, erschreckt all strëfflich gail,
          mit wirdiklichem hail.
          Si hat den breis in meinem herzen ewiklich
          für alle, die ich ie gesach;
          ir wandel, weis ist wol so reich,
          das si wenndt ungemach,
          süsslich an welich ach.

II   Freu dich, du weltlich creatur,
                das dir all mass, tün, lass recht wol anstat,
                Und du nach menschlicher natur
                loblichen zart von art keuschliche wat
                besitzt an missetat.
                Dick, smel, kürz, leng, von höch zu tal, so ist ir leib
                waidlich possnieret unverhönt,
                und dein gemeng von amplick, weib,
                blaich, weiss, durch rot getrönt,
                für alle maid verkrönt.

III   Junckfrau, durch all dein köstlich er,
                solt ich von got an spot des wierdig sein,
                So wolt ich doch nicht wünschen mer,
                wann das ich möcht, getöcht neur wesen dein,
                recht als ain gsläfelein.
                Erst wolt ich geuden, gailich schallen, singen hel
                von meiner frauen, der ich wër,
                und die mit freuden herz, müt, leib, sel
                wol hailen mag an swër,
                mit wort, werch und gepär.

Its rhyme scheme follows the pattern ababbcdcdd. (It will be noted that *ewiklich* rhymes with *reich*.) Each strophe therefore falls into two identical parts so far as the rhyme scheme is concerned, although the parts are otherwise unlike. It is noteworthy that the first half of each strophe has a subsidiary rhyming pattern. Lines 2 and 4 in each strophe each contain rhyming words separated by one syllable (*war/klar, verdeckt/ erschreckt*, and so on). Lines 1 and 3 have no internal rhyme but are connected in all three strophes by the presence of a word ending in *-ich* (*adeliche/keuschlich, weltlich/menschlicher, köstlich/nicht*). These words are not, of course, rhymes, but in combination with the internal rhymes already mentioned, they show the close combination between the pairs in the first half and the fact that the last line is a coda.

The second halves of the three strophes show no such pattern. It is true that there is considerable assonance and alliteration within the lines (*wandel/weis/reich, süsslich/welich/ach, blaich/weiss, rot/gekrönt, geuden/gailich, schallen/singen*), but these are sound effects of the types already mentioned, not patterned alliteration. By these means Oswald distinguishes carefully between the two halves of each strophe. In the first he uses a strict pattern, with little free alliteration; in the second a simple pattern with much free alliteration. The meaning also follows this division. The first half is in every case praise of his "adeliche maid," with few sensual figures. The second halves are highly sensuous, full of graphic impressions (note the *frequentatio* on the sixth line of each of the last two strophes and the use of impressive monosyllables in many lines). In this poem, then, the internal assonance-alliteration pattern serves a very clear formal purpose.

When Oswald uses a rhyme scheme in which several rhyming lines succeed one another, he is prone to relieve the succession by the lavish use of alliteration. In poem number 39, for example, the rhyme scheme is aaabcccbdede, a common enough pattern. But in the *a* and *c* lines there is a great deal of alliteration: *sünd/schuld* in strophe I and *sünd/ sünd/sünd/tün/günstlich* in strophe 3, to quote only the most obvious examples. Both this poem and number 78 are serious poems. When Oswald uses unrelieved monorhyme or monorhyme combined with internal rhyme, the effect is almost always intended to be comic. The phenomenon is easily observed in poem number 45:

> Wer machen well sein peutel ring,
> und im desselben wolgeling,
> der frag den weg gen Überling,
> da gelten vierzen pfifferling
> fünfzen schilling
> der Costnitzer geslagen;

But it reaches its peak, if such a term may be used in connection with a poem like this, in poem number 20. It is a long poem, and there is room to quote only one strophe, although I am doubtful whether "strophe" may legitimately be used of such a monster.

> Es seusst dort her von orient
> der wind, levant ist er genent;
> durch India er wol erkennt,
> in Suria ist er behend,
> zu Kriechen er nit widerwent,

durch Barbaria das gelent,
Granaten hat er bald errent,
Portugal, Ispanie erbrent.
uberall die werlt von ort zu end
regniert der edel element;
der tag in hat zu bott gesennt.
der nach im durch das firmament
schon dringt zu widerstreit ponent.
des freut sich dort in occident
das norbögnische geschlëchte.
Den sturm erhort ain freulin zart,
do es mit armes banden hart
mit liebem lust verslossen ward.
si sprach: "ich hör die widerpart,
der tag die nacht mit schein bekart,
wach auf, mein hort! sich hat geschart
der sterne glast von himels gart,
wachter, ich spür ain valsche wart,
dein leib pringt mich in jamers art.
ach wicht! wer hat dich das gelart,
das du mich pringst in sendes mart,
davon mein herz in laid erstart,
es müsst mich reuen hie und dart,
ob im missling mit hinevart;
das pringt dein snödes geträchte."
 Zwar si began in drucken,
 zucken aus dem slaff,
 freuntlich an sich smucken,
 rucken ane straff,
 das er began zu krachen,
 wachen, sunder swachen
 machen lieplich zaff.

Everything is in a breathless hurry and all to tell us that dawn is coming, a beautiful parody of the opening of a *Tagelied*. The effect is achieved, of course, by the fourteen-times-repeated final syllable. Oswald is far from attempting to relieve the monotony. On the contrary, he reinforces it by the alliteration of similar syllables—*wint, levant, India, regniert, edel,* and so forth, and he continues the technique when the rhyming syllable changes to *-art, -armes, sprach, tag, nacht, wach, hat, glast, wachter,* and so forth. The refrain plays an exceedingly complicated sound game, which is best illustrated by setting out the important sounds.

I	a	an	i	uck

```
I          a    an   i    uck
           uck  au   aff
           f    an   ucken
           ucken an  aff
               an   achen
           achen un  achen
           achen     aff

II         un   im   itzen
           itzen in  und
           in   ie  itzen
           itzen     und
               o  iessen
           iessen än  iessen
           iessen on  unt

III        ie   in   innen
           innen in  ans
           ei   in  inne
           inne      ans
           ei   ei  achen
           achen     achen
           achen i  ans
```

Two main rhymes run through the poem, locking tail-to-head-to-tail-to-head in each case. The other line endings are connected by a different rhyme, which in the first two strophes is joined to a persistently repeated word (*an* in the first, *in* in the second). The play with monorhymes in each strophe has been succeeded by head and tail rhymes in rapid succession, with the middle of the line assonanced. Oswald regards this hurried pattern of monorhyme and assonance as comic and uses it accordingly.

A desire to obtain comic effects explains a great deal about even the more formal patterns of Oswald's poetry. Let us examine at least a part of poem number 16.

"Ich spür ain lufft aus külem tufft,
das mich wol dunckt in meiner vernunft
wie er genennet, kennet sei nordoste.
Ich, wachter, sag, mich prüfft der tag
uns künftig sein aus vinsterm hag;
ich sich, vergich die morgenrot her glosten.
Die voglin klingen überal,
galander, lerchen, zeisel, droschel, nachtigal,
auf perg, in tal hat sich ir gesangk erschellet.
Leit iemant hie in güter acht,
der sich in freuden hat geniet die langen nacht,
derselb betracht, das er sich mer gesellet."
    Die junckfrau hett verslaffen,
    der knab wacht lützel bas,
    si rüfften baide waffen
    all über des tages hass.
    das freulin schalt in sere:
    "her tag, ir künnt nicht ere
    bewaren inn der mass."

Throughout the poem the alliteration-rhyme scheme is as follows:

	a		a
			a
	b	b	c
		d	d
			d
	e	e	c
			f
			f
	f		g
			h
			h
	h		g

It will be observed that here, as so often in Oswald's poetry, the rhymes form a triangular pattern, with two end rhymes and a word in the interior of the line rhyming. There is almost always one word in the interior of the line which at least assonances with the rhyming sound, so that there is a broken effect, a quick, chopping rhythm. If these triangular rhyme patterns were the only feature of the poem, there would be little reason for comment, but the pattern is complicated by numerous additions. The *a* rhyming sound in the first strophe is *ufft*. This assonances with the *ü* of *spür* and *külen* in the first line and *dünckt* in the second, so that the cumulative effect is much greater than the rhyme scheme would indicate. The same sound appears again in line 4 (*prüfft*) and line 5 (*künftig*). But in line 5 there also begins another assonance pattern with the sound *in* (*vinstern, voglin, klingen*). In strophe II the pattern varies from that of strophe I but is just as effective (*schicklin/im, hin/hendlin, hin/freulin,* and so on) and varies again in strophe III (*horn/hort, gast/gelast*). The whole poem is filled with repeated and shaded sounds, so that the reader becomes almost hypnotized by the constant repetition. The poem is, of course, a *Tagelied,* and the discrepancy between the reluctance of the lovers to part at dawn and the rhymes that hurry them along has a totally parodistic effect. Poem number 33, also a *Tagelied,* achieves similar effects in a slightly different way. The poem has an extremely complicated assonance-rhyme scheme:

Ain tunckle farb von occident
mich senlichen erschrecket,
Seid ich ir darb und lig ellend
des nachtes ungedecket.
Die mir zu vleiss mit ermlein weiss und hendlin gleiss
kan freuntlich zu ir smucken,
Die ist so lang, das ich von pang in meim gesang
mein klag nicht mag verdrucken.
Von strecken krecken mir all bain,
wenn ich die lieb beseuffte,
Die mir mein gier neur weckt allain,
darzü meins vatters teuchte.

Durch wincken wanck ich mich verker
des nachtes ungeslauffen,
Gierlich gedanck mir nahent ferr
mit unhillichem waffen.
wenn ich mein hort an seinem ort nicht vind all dort,
wie offt ich nach im greiffe,

So ist neur, ach, vil ungemach, feur in dem tach,
Als ob mich brenn der reiffe.
und winden, binden sunder sail
tüt si mich dann gen tage.
Ir mund all stund weckt mir die gail
mit seniklicher klage.

Also vertreibe ich, liebe Gret,
die nacht bis an den morgen.
Dein zarter lieb mein herz durchgeet,
das sing ich unverborgen,
Kom, höchster schatz! mich schreckt ain ratz mit grossem tratz,
davon ich dick erwachen,
Die mir kain rü lat spät noch frü, lieb, dorzu tü
damit das bettlin krache!
Die freud geud ich auf hohem stül,
wenn das mein herz bedencket,
Das mich hoflich mein schöner bül
gen tag freuntlichen schrencket.

	a	b
		c
	a	b
		c
d	d	d
		e
f	f	f
g	g	e
h	h	k
		l
m	m	k
		l

All the strophes follow this scheme, except that in some cases alliteration is substituted for rhyme, for example in the eighth lines (*klag/mag, ob/brenn, damit/das*), and here again there is considerable supporting alliteration (*mir/mein/gier, neur/feur*). There are few words that are not part of the sound pattern.

After this demonstration that Oswald uses such schemes for comic and parodistic effect, it is more than a little disconcerting to encounter a poem like number 31. For the pattern here is remarkably like the one just discussed.

I   Der oben swebt und niden hebt,
             der vor und hinden, neben strebt
             und ewig lebt, ie was an anefange,
             Der alt, der jung, und der von sprung
             trilitzscht gefasst in ainlitz zung
             an misshellung, mit unbegriffner strange,
             Der strenklich starb und was nicht tod,
             der keuschlich ward emphangen und an alle not
             geboren rot, weiss durch ain junckfrau schöne,
             Der manig wunder hat gestifft,
             der hell er brach, den tiefel dorin ser vergifft,
             getült, geschifft al wurz durch stammes tröne.

II   Dem offen sein all herzen schrein,
             grob, tadelhäfftig, swach, güt, vein,
             das er dorin sicht allerlai gedenke,
             dem tün und lan ist undertan,
             die himel steren, sunn, der man,
             der erden plan, mensch, tier, all wasser rencke,
             Auss dem all kunst geflossen ist,
             von dem, der aller creatur durch spähen list
             zu jeder frist ir zierhait würckt, schon eusset,
             Dem alle tier, zam und ouch wild,
             hie danckber sein, das er den samen hat gebildt,
             der narung milt gar waideleich vergreusset.

III   Der himel, erd, gar unversert,
             hat undersetzt an grundes herd,
             das wasser kert dorin durch fremde rünste,—
             Der wunder zal vil tusent mal
             wër mer ze singen überal
             mit reichem schal, so hindern mich die künste—,
             Der mir die sel klar geben hat,
             leib, er und güt, vernufft und kristenliche wat:
             der geb mir rat, das ich im also dancke,
             Da mit ich all mein veind verpaw

baid hie und dort, das mich ir kainer nicht verhau.
O keuschlich frau, dein hilf mir dorzu schrancke!

Once again we have the pattern of head-to-tail rhyme, and again there is no lack of supporting alliteration (*oben/niden/hinden/neben, strencklich/starb* in strophe I, for example). It would thus appear that this serious religious poem is written in the same comic-parodistic vein as those already studied. In fact this is hardly likely, for Oswald keeps his serious works notably free of such tricks. The key lies in the approach to this song in praise of Christ and the Virgin. The purpose is, as the first line shows, to identify the Incarnate Christ with the created world (*Der oben swebt und niden hebt*). Although God, Christ lived and died in the created world, and Oswald uses the techniques of graphic description of that world which he employed in so many other poems. It is thus that we can explain the piling up of adjectives of physical description in the second line of strophe II and the detailed description of the created world in strophes II and III, which is deliberately reminiscent of Genesis. Throughout the poem Oswald is able to emphasize the double nature of Christ by the employment of rhyme and assonance of contrasting characteristics and actions. In other words, he uses the techniques of earthiness to emphasize the spirit.

The patterns of the poems just discussed, although showing considerable sophistication, were relatively simple, characterized as they were by head and tail rhyme and by additional alliteration within the line, with the occasional use of vertical alliteration. Oswald was capable of patterns much more complicated than these. I shall quote only the first strophe of poem number 106 to illustrate the general pattern:

Nempt war der schönen plüde, früde!
müde ist der kalde winder.
kinder, schickt eu zu dem tanz!
glanz zieret sich lustlich des maien tenne
Durch manger hendlin farbe, garbe,
marbe würzlin, grüne gräsli,
wäsli mit den plümlin gel.
hel singt die nachtigal weit für die henne.
Die droschel hat ain wett getan
mit ainem alten rappen

zu tichten auff des maien pan,
und gilt ain junge kappen.
vil stolzer maide wellen dran,
das wisst, ir röschen knappen.

Here we find that the basic rhyme scheme is complicated by the use of double rhyming words:

	a	a
a	b
b	c
c	d
	e	e
e	f
f	g
g	d

The *Abgesang* has normal alternating end rhyme. The *Aufgesang* thus consists of two *Stollen*, the first line of each of which has double rhyme at the end and within which all lines are linked by head-to-tail rhyme. But the *Aufgesang* is also remarkable for the obvious effort to associate alliteration with the rhyme: *kalde/winder/kinder, glanz/zieret/sich/ lustlich, würzlin/grüne/gräsli/wäsli, helfe/gelfe/tapferlich/gestalt,* and many others. This is a clear case of progressive alliteration coupled with a rhyming pattern, and the intention to construct such a pattern is made all the more clear by its complete absence in the *Abgesang*.

The urge to produce a heavily alliterated pattern is perhaps best exemplified by poem number 86.

I   O phalzgraf Ludewig
           bei Rein so vein, dein steig
           geit braite, schraitte tugent gross,
           kainer dein genoss
           dir nicht geleichen mag.
           hör mich, was ich dir sag!
           sich klärlich, bärlich vindet das
           nach adelicher mass,
           Die rürstu, fürstu in stëtem schilt
           durch manhait, weisshait warhafft milt,
           ouch freuen dich die frauen, permafoi,

       hort ich von deim getruen
       gemaheln von Sophoi.

II   Ich rüm dich, Haidelwerg,
       lob, oben auf dem perg,
       das schöne, fröne mündlin rot
       da zeren mûss und brot
       mit züchten wolgemüt.
       ir er ist ser behüt
       durch Metzlin, Ketzlin, Kädrichin,
       Agnes und Engichin,
       Der jugent, tugent wolgeziert
       mit wandel, handel ungefiert.
       das lob ich got, den milden, was ich kan,
       das er also kan bilden
       schön kindlichin wolgetan.

III   Do ich den Neckar koss,
       der bach gemach nicht floss
       in Rein, der Main, darzu die Nau
       umb Pingen. Neckerau,
       Dein scheren ungenetzt
       der taschen maschen setzt,
       an rûff schûff ich mir güt gemach
       zu Manhain, Bacherach.
       Unfröstlich, köstlich mein da ward
       gepflegen, engegen von dem lieben bart,
       der mich hat schon gedecket mit füchsen swër,
       durch märder ser erschrecket;
       das spil louff mir nicht lër.

This lighthearted song of praise is exactly suited to Oswald's style. Its pattern is as follows:

```
                     a
         b     b     a
         c     c     d
                     d
                     e
         f     f     e
```

```
    g      g      h
                  h
    k      k      1
    m      m      1
    n      n      o
                  p
                  o
```

Yet this rhyme scheme, complex though it is, shows only a small part
of the sound play. In the first four lines the sounds *i*, *ei*, and *ai* occur
no less than eleven times out of a total of twenty-five vowels. This is a
very typical Oswald opening, an attempt to shock the listener into attention. But the pattern is continued. Out of a total of twenty-six
vowels, the closely associated sounds represented by *i* and *ei* occur
eleven times in the next four lines. The proportion is suspiciously close,
especially since the unstressed *e* of *adelicher* in line 8 may well have
been slurred. In the *Abgesang*, the pattern of alliteration extends to
consonants: *rürstu/furstu, steten/schilt, weisshait/warhafft, freuen/
frauen/foi.* Although assonance is by no means lacking in the other two
strophes, as can be seen in such examples as *ir/er/ist/ser, Metzlin/
Ketzlin/Kädrichin, Agnes/Engichin,* it does not appear in anything
like so complex a pattern as in the first strophe, and this is only one
example of a very common feature of Oswald's poetry—that he took
many more pains with his first strophes than with subsequent ones.

I would like to examine one more highly structured poem, number
91, and again we shall have to confine quotation to the first strophe.

> Freuntlicher blick
> wundet ser meins herzens schrein
> mit ainem scharpfen zain,
> zwai öglin rain,
> lauter, klar und vein,
> ein, sein gewaltig mein.
> Auss slauffes schrick,
> vil gedenck, melancholi,
> dicke mir wonen bei,
> zetter ich schrei
> nach der edlen drei,

> ei, das si bei mir sei!
> Ir günstlich grüss
> von dem mündlin süss
> mit unmüss
> mir pringt senlich büss
> baide, tag und nacht,
> so ich betracht und acht,
> das mich liederlichen umbfacht
> ermlin macht.
> Mit hertem druck
> kürlich zu ir smuck
> und mich tuck,
> das si nicht enzuck,
> bis ir rotter mund
> auf sleust den punt verwunt,
> das si maisterlichen ain grund
> schaffen kund.

The basic rhyme is simple. The first line rhymes with the seventh, and the lines between all rhyme with one another. There follow rhyming groups of five, four, four, four, and four lines, a total of twenty-eight. Such a scheme is simple to the point of monotony, especially in a strophe of such length, but it serves as a frame for a complex series of assonances. The rhyming sound *ei* of lines 2 to 6 occurs no less than ten times in the first six lines and seven times more in lines 8 to 12, even if we do not count the *i* sounds that are allowed to rhyme with it. It may be noted at this point that there is head-to-tail rhyme in lines 5 and 6, 11 and 12, in all strophes except between lines 11 and 12 in strophe II, where I think we must assume that Oswald regards the assonance *verlän/von* as sufficient for his pattern. In lines 13 to 16 the rhyming vowel *ü* occurs six times, seven if we include *u*. The internal sound repetition continues in the following groups—*tag/nacht/betracht/acht* and *druck/kürlich/smuck/tuck*, although with a decreasing number of vowel assonances. There is no question of an internal rhyme pattern here, for the vowel assonances are not repeated in the same pattern in the second and third strophes. The second rhyming sound *a* occurs only once in lines 2 to 6 outside the rhyming pattern—and that in the head-to-tail position already mentioned—but the rhyming sound of lines

16 to 20, again *ai*, occurs no less than nine times, and the *en* sound of
the last rhyme of the strophe, seven times. In the third strophe the
rhyming sounds are by no means so obvious on the printed page, because Oswald is assonancing the *ai/ei/i/ie* group.

In addition to this complicated assonance pattern, we may note the
supporting alliteration. In the heavily assonanced lines at the beginning
of the first strophe, there is hardly any consonant alliteration. It begins
in line 13 (*günstlich/grüss, mündlin/mit/unmüss*), but the first
strophe in general shows little alliteration. In the second, where, as
we noted, the vowel assonance declines, the alliteration increases (*selig/
selden/sehen, sinne/seid, deines/leibes, werfen/wil*. Lines 14 and 15
seem to be favorites for the alliteration-assonance pattern (*mündlin
süss/mit unmüss, wilden wag/tüglich tag, waisst wol wo/hab also*).
In the third strophe, much of the alliteration is vertical (*Ach/las/was,
raine/raine/mein/mein/dein/verhailen/kain/allaine/meins/dein*, and
so on in almost every line).

There are several linguistic curiosities among Oswald's poems, in
which he shows off his skill in various languages by writing macaronic
verse. Fortunately he is usually kind enough to provide an *expositio*
for the benefit of those of us who are not so learned. An examination
of these poems shows that he is just as determined to produce alliterative and assonantal effects in these poems as in his German ones, proof
indeed, if any be needed, of the conscious nature of his sound patterns.
Here is poem number 69:

> Do fraig amors,
> adiuva me!
> ma lot, mein ors,
> na moi sercce,
> rennt mit gedanck,
> frau, puräti.
> Eck lopp, ick slapp,
> vel quo vado,
> wesegg mein krap
> ne dirs dobro.
> iu gslaff ee franck
> merschi vois gri.

Teutsch, welschisch mach!
franzoisch wach!
ungrischen lach!
brot windisch bach!
flemming so krach!
latein die sibend sprach.
Mille schenna,
ime, man gür,
peromnia
des leibes spür.
Cenza befiu
mit gschoner war
dut servirai,
pur zschätti gaiss,
nem tudem frai
kain falsche rais.
gott wett wol, twiw
eck de amar.
De mit mundesch,
Margaritha well,
exprofundes
das tün ich snell.
datt löff, draga
griet, per ma foi!
in recommisso
diors et not
mi ti commando,
wo ich trott,
jambre, twoia,
allopp mi troi.

The numerous sound effects are immediately apparent—*am/ad/me/ mein/moi, eck/ick, lopp/slapp, vel/vado/wesegg*, and so on. The second strophe plays with the *mi* sound as the first does with *ma* and continues with *dut/pur, nem/tudem, welt/wol*. It is quite clear from the interpretation provided by Oswald that meaning is a secondary matter in this poem. He has set it up so that even the foreign words conform to his sound patterns.

What conclusions can we draw about Oswald's poetry from these studies? Firstly we should note that he does not use the techniques of patterned alliteration and assonance in all his works. In serious moral and religious poetry he is very sparing of these effects. When he does use them, it is almost always to produce a sound pattern, much less frequently to reinforce meaning by appropriate sounds. In fact it is not too much to say that a very large number of Oswald's poems are primarily studies in sound patterns rather than poems in which we expect to be able to trace continuous meaning. It is largely this factor of sound pattern which is responsible for the well-known difficulty in interpreting his poetry. He is very prone to use unusual or nonsense words, provided that they will fit his sound pattern. We should also notice that he uses these sound patterns for comic effect, again not because of any comic meaning but because of the—to him at least—amusing sounds that he could produce. In this essay I have been able to do no more than make a start on a very complicated question, but I have said enough, I hope, to show that it is often to sound patterns that we must turn in medieval poetry rather than make attempts to extract meaning from repetitions of worn-out clichés.

minnesang: some metrical problems

BY HUBERT HEINEN

We must look to the marriage of metrics and musicology for answers in the controversial study of the meter of medieval German poetry. Although Heusler[1] in his attempt to find a unifying tendency in German poetry rejected the early attempts at such a marriage, it has become increasingly clear that explanations of the great variety of metrical phenomena cannot hope to be adequate if they ignore the findings of the musicologists.

The studies by Gennrich, Spanke, Jammers, Husmann, Taylor, Aarburg, and others have demonstrated the significance of music as a formative element in *Minnesang*. We now realize the importance of contrafacture and can recognize the compatibility of as well as the difference between borrowing Medieval Latin, French, and Provençal rhythmical patterns and continuing older Germanic ones.[2] Heusler's anachronistic measures in 2/4 time no longer dominate. On the contrary, we may assume that the greater part of *Minnesang* was written to melodies that were modeled on or borrowed from Medieval Latin, Provençal, or French ones. These in turn were probably largely modal in their rhythms.

Kippenberg has been able to make the concept of modal rhythms for monodic song questionable, and his criticism, coupled with the conclusions of Bertau, who doubts the presence of such rhythms in the *Leiche* he studies, reminds us to be careful. Still, it is reasonable to assume that the modes which were later formalized in theoretical writings and polyphonic settings in France were present in some form, perhaps a freer one, in the melodies of the trouvères and troubadours copied and imitated by the German *Minnesänger*. In the work of many

[1] See the bibliographic note and selected bibliography for this and other studies mentioned.

[2] These "Germanic" patterns are probably not direct descendents of alliterative verse, but rather reworkings of Medieval Latin accentual meters to suit the stress patterns common to Germanic verse.

poets the local traditions exist alongside the foreign ones, and we may assume that contamination and confusion of the various traditions arose. As far as we know, all metrical traditions were transmitted by imitation of what a poet heard.[3] The stylized foreign rhythms would quite likely be more or less radically modified in being borrowed. As a means of reference, however, we may assume that the following modal rhythms were used in medieval German verse: 1 ⌣ x; 2 x́ -; 3 ⌐ x́ -[⌣ x x̀ -]; 5 ⌐ ∟; 6 ⌣ - -.[4] In addition, there was apparently a local rhythm available which one might schematize as follows: a x́ a x́ a x́[a x́ (x)]: |.[5] Heusler assumes this rhythm to have been isochronic, but it is more reasonable to suppose that relative equality of the time intervals between stresses resulted from and is characteristic of generally regular verse.[6] *Minnesang* in this tradition seems regular enough for us to assume a rather consistent beat.

Werner Schröder denies the existence of such a traditional pattern in long lines with internal rhyme[7] and similarily rejects the theory that the rhymed couplets, as he considers them, were sung. Although the

---

[3] There seems to have been no theory of metrics in Germany until the poets of the Teutonic Order of Knights attempted to create one (to replace a lost or hazy tradition?), and even this attempt apparently remained a regional oddity.

[4] If one assumes that x is a basic unit, then - is roughly twice as long and ∟ is roughly three times as long. It is not impossible that the modes, as they appear in Germany at least, were originally simply arrangements of longer and shorter notes, without the strict 1 : 2 : 3 relationship suggested here. Borrowings from Gregorian chant would probably not have provided the poet with rhythmical patterns at all, so that for such borrowings he would most likely turn for metrical guidance to other traditions.

[5] The *a* here represents anything from no syllable (with certain restrictions) to a number which varies according to period and poet from one (or two short syllables) to perhaps five. The square brackets indicate that the last stress may be paused. This general pattern holds true, I feel, whether one accepts Maurer's long-line hypothesis or not.

[6] Jammer's distinction between musical measure and metrical freedom seems to me to be inadequate, for both music and verse may be roughly isochronic, or the music may lack rhythmic order and the meter may be irregular. Of course, regularity of meter may have been caused by the adoption of measured music.

[7] The end-rhymed long lines found in the *Kürenberger-(Nibelungen-) Strophe* are not, strictly speaking, local, but rather characteristically Austrian, at least from around 1150 to 1230.

Early Middle High German verse he and Maurer are considering is epic poetry, Maurer (who postulates long lines as schematized above) does hold that it is strophic and traces it into *Minnesang*. Schröder's scansion of this verse is interesting and provocative, and we must be grateful to him for causing us to re-examine our basic assumptions. However, he makes two assumptions which are extremely dubious. He assumes that it is possible to make metrics completely objective, and as one consequence of this assumption he proposes that a word stressed in one line must be stressed in all other lines. It seems rather doubtful that the degree of objectivity which Schröder strives to establish can ever be attained. As for his prosodic rule, there would be no other German verse to which it would apply, not to Otfrid's nor to that of the High Middle Ages, certainly not to *Knüttelvers* or the Baroque Alexandrine, so that it would seem quite unlikely that we should scan Early Middle High German verse differently from all other.

If one cannot hope for objectivity in metrics, what can one hope for? Two of the many problems discussed by students of medieval German metrics are cadence and rhythmic pattern, and a discussion of these two points can serve to illustrate what sort of results one might reasonably expect.

Schirmer scans the following strophe by Walther von der Vogelweide as 4wa, 4wb|4wa, 4wb||4mKorn, 4wc, 4wc—all lines dactylic according to the text in the edition of Carl von Kraus. I prefer Maurer's text (Maurer 61 = [110,13]), which follows the manuscript tradition more closely:

> Wol mich der stunde, daz ich sie erkande,
> diu mir den lip und den muot hat betwungen,
> sit deich die sinne so gar an sie wande,
> der si mich hat mit ir güete verdrungen.
> Daz ich von ir gescheiden niht enkan:
> daz hat ir schoene und ir güete gemachet
> und ir roter munt, der so lieplichen lachet.
>
> Ich han den muot und die sinne gewendet
> an die vil reinen, die lieben, die guoten.
> Daz müez uns beiden wol werden volendet,
> swes ich getar an ir hulde gemuoten.

Swaz ich zer werlde fröiden ie gewan:
daz hat ir schoene und ir güete gemachet
und ir roter mund, der so lieplichen lachet.

The best reading of the first four and last two lines is in the third mode,
with the fifth line (with anacrusis) in the second.

$$| \acute{L} \, x - | \acute{L} \, \dot{x} - | \acute{L} \, \dot{x} - | \acute{L} \, \dot{x} \, (_\wedge) \quad [4 \text{ times}]$$
$$x \, | \, ^\epsilon x \, | \, ^\epsilon x \, | \, ^\epsilon x \, | \, ^\epsilon x \, | \, ^\epsilon _\wedge$$
$$| \acute{L} \, x - | \acute{L} \, \dot{x} - | \acute{L} \, \dot{x} - | \acute{L} \, \dot{x} _\wedge$$
$$| \, ^\epsilon x \, \dot{x} - | \acute{L} \, \dot{x} - | \acute{L} \, \dot{x} - | \acute{L} \, \dot{x} _\wedge$$

It is possible, however, that Walther employed some rhythmic pattern
related to the fifth or sixth mode for all lines.

5	6
$\| \, ^\epsilon x x \, \| \, ^\epsilon x x \, \| \, ^\epsilon x x \, \| \, ^\epsilon x \, (_\wedge) \quad [4 \text{ times}]$	$\| \, \acute{x} x x \, \| \, \acute{x} x x \, \| \, \acute{x} x x \, \| \, \acute{x} x \, (_\wedge)$
$x \, \| \, ^\epsilon - \, \| \, ^\epsilon - \, \| \, ^\epsilon - \, \| \, ^\epsilon - \, \| \, ^\epsilon _\wedge$	$x \, \| \, ^\epsilon x \, \| \, ^\epsilon x \, \| \, ^\epsilon x \, \| \, ^\epsilon x \, \| \, ^\epsilon _\wedge$
$\| \, ^\epsilon x x \, \| \, ^\epsilon x x \, \| \, ^\epsilon x x \, \| \, ^\epsilon x _\wedge$	$\| \, \acute{x} x x \, \| \, \acute{x} x x \, \| \, \acute{x} x x \, \| \, \acute{x} x$
$\| \, \acute{x} x x x \, \| \, ^\epsilon x x \, \| \, ^\epsilon x x \, \| \, ^\epsilon x _\wedge$	$x \, \| \, \acute{x} x x \, \| \, \acute{x} x x \, \| \, \acute{x} x x \, \| \, \acute{x} x _\wedge [8]$

The fact that most editors have found it necessary to emend the text to
produce pure dactyls can serve as a reminder that emendations for
metrical reasons should be made with great care. Some texts are obviously corrupt, but much of the metrical smoothness and consistency
found in our standard texts may well not represent the intent of the
author, but rather that of the editor. The manuscript tradition and
Maurer's use of it give the fifth, transitional line a rhythmic twist which
suits its function.[9] Maurer probably realized this in establishing his

---

[8] I assume here that $\acute{L} \, L$ is equivalent to $^\epsilon -$ (so also Taylor) and that the
latter can be changed to $^\epsilon x x$ or $\acute{x} x x x$ without losing its basic character.
Similarly, I have equated $^\epsilon - -$ with $\acute{x} x x$ (with Taylor) and postulated a
variation of the latter as $^\epsilon x$, which is, of course, practically identical with the
first mode. All of these changes are possible if we hold to an oral (aural)
transmission of the rhythmic patterns. Note that $_\wedge$ represents a rest. A paused
stress is represented as $\acute{\wedge}$.

[9] Maurer himself emends the second and fifth lines of the second strophe to
produce the text we have here. Perhaps the fifth line as transmitted ("Swaz
ich fröiden zer werlde ie gewan") can be regarded as a five-stress alternating
one without anacrusis or elision of the hiatus *e* in *werlde* but with a three-
syllable second measure, as such a legitimate (?) variation of the corresponding
line in the first strophe.

text, for he points to a similar phenomenon in a study of the poetry of
Heinrich von Morungen. Hugo Kuhn uses comparable arguments in
rejecting the textual emendations made in "Rífe und ànehánc hàt die
héidè betwúngèn," attributed to Gottfried von Neifen, in order to retain the third mode recognizable in the manuscript tradition.

In another poem by Walther, the question of cadence presents itself.
The first strophe follows (Maurer 93 = [64,31]):

> Owe, hovelichez singen,
> daz dich ungefüege dœne
> solten ie ze hove verdringen!
> daz die schiere got gehœne!
> Owe daz din wirde also geliget!
> des sint alle dine friunde unfro.
> daz muoz also sin, nu si also!
> fro Unfuoge, ir habt gesiget.

Schirmer scans this poem 5ka, 5kb| 5ka, 5kb|| 5mc, 5md, 5md, 5sc.
I find the scansion 4wa, 4wb|4wa, 4wb||5mc, 5md, 5md, 5sc (?) more
likely. Although one cannot prove either scansion, one can survey the
opinions about the choice of cadence.

(a) When anacrusis (*Auftakt* or *Vorsenkung*) follows, one tends
to read the cadence (*schwer-*)*klingend* (double-stressed): | ́ | x́ : x |.
When there is no anacrusis, one often decides for feminine (*weiblich*)
cadence: | x́ x : |. Plenio, Heusler, Maurer, and Schirmer make this
assumption for all but dactylic verse; Bertau rejects it.[10]

(b) Heusler, Taylor, and Bertau agree that lines, or at least periods
(several lines together), should have an even number of measures.
Schirmer rejects this assumption.

(c) In a framework of four-beat verse, "three-beat" lines should be
read as four-beat ones with either double-stressed (k) or *stumpf* (last
beat in the pause = paused) cadence. Often one is led to choose feminine cadence, as Schirmer does generally, if this choice results in four-
beat lines.[11]

---

[10] *Sangverslyrik*, p. 52; he partially reinstates it as a working hypothesis on
p. 106.

[11] Schröder assumes that one has only double-stressed and masculine cadence
in Early Middle High German verse. This seems unlikely, since the assumption

(d) If we have the music, one can occasionally determine the cadence from musical parallels. This observation of Bertau's holds true primarily for the later *Leiche*.

(e) The paused cadence(s), which may be musically a one-bar rest or a note stretched over two bars, may occur at the end of a longer structural unit, in some cases after a line shorter by one beat than the preceding one (see [c] above), in any case, however, after a clear syntactic break.

These guidelines are in general accepted and applied by Schirmer, but for this poem he chooses to deny them all.

The chief reason for Schirmer's scansion, which he shares with Hatto, is his conviction that the number of beats of the strophe and its parts must be significant, even symbolic. For this purpose, dozens of numbers can be regarded as significant or symbolic, but not all. I agree with Kippenberg and Bertau in rejecting number symbolism and numerical composition as a tool in metrics and textual criticism. It is unlikely that Walther, Wolfram, or the other poets counted beats (they were probably not even aware of them as countable entities). It is still more unlikely that they counted them symbolically or planned numerical patterns by including unorganic beats in the pauses after (and before) certain lines.

Although the number four is not symbolic, four-beat lines do predominate in *Minnesang*. However, Hugo Kuhn suggests that one should scan verse by Gottfried von Neifen (e.g., XIV and XX) with generally three-beat lines, feminine and masculine cadences, rather than four-beat lines with double-stressed and paused cadences, as von Kraus and Heusler scan them. Kuhn gives two reasons for his scansion: a long series of double-stressed cadences is unbearably monotonous, and Gottfried's verse is in the Northern French, not in the German, tradition. Since the metrical and stylistic evidence supports the four-beat scansion, I feel that an aesthetic argument proves little. After all,

---

is part of his larger theory of metrics which I feel to be dubious. The position which he supports that the double-stressed cadence be considered a variant of masculine cadence with frequent extended rhyme is well worth considering, although this does present difficulties which cannot be discussed here.

the content and syntactic structure of the verse in question is also monotonous. The question of tradition provides a more substantial argument. Still, Kuhn considers the *Büttnerlied*, which may have been written by Gottfried, to exhibit a mixture of both formal traditions, and the same may be true of the poems in question.[12]

Up to this point, we have been forced to speculate, but for one poem by Neidhart von Reuenthal we possess a melody transmitted in a rudimentary mensural notation. Here we can, to a certain extent, test our speculations (Wiessner/Fischer, Sommerlied 23):

> Blozen wir den anger ligen sahen,
> end uns diu liebe zit begunde nahen,
> daz die bluomen drungen durch den kle
> aber als e.
> heide diust mit rosen nu bevangen:
>> den tuot der sumer wol, niht we.

> Droschel, nahtigal die hœrt man singen,
> von ir schalle berc unt tal erklingen:
> sie vreunt sich gegen der lieben sumerzit,
> diu uns git
> vreuden vil und liehter ougenweide.
>> diu heide wünneclichen lit.

> Sprach ein maget: "die wisen wellent touwen.
> megt ir an dem sumer wunder schouwen?
> die boume, die den winder stuonden val,
> über al
> sint si niuwes loubes worden riche:
>> dar under singent nahtigal.[13]

---

[12] Kuhn and others have come to regard the double-stressed and paused cadences with great suspicion, and this attitude is apparently reflected in the arguments and cadence formulas of *Minnesangs Wende*. The time is ripe for all evidence and arguments for and against the existence of these types of cadence to be assembled and weighed. Perhaps it will be possible then to reach a consensus of opinion.

[13] Only the first three strophes are reproduced here. The normalized text may have oversimplified the meter, but any return to variant readings would be arbitrary without an extensive study of the manuscript traditions.

If I were confronted with this text without the music, I would probably schematize its form as follows:

x́ x x́ x x́ x x.x́ x x́ x
(x)x́.x x́.x x́ x x́ x x́ x
(x)x́.x x́ x x́ x x́ x x́
x́ x x́
x́ x.x́ x x́ x x́ x x́ x   x x́ x x́ x x́ x x́[14]

Gennrich and Taylor have given us transcriptions of the poem in the first rhythmic mode based on the use of apparent *semibreves* and *minimae* in the manuscript.

Taylor	Gennrich
| ⁺x | ¹x | ⁺x | ¹x | Ḻ | ¹	| x́xx | ⁺x | ⁺x | ⁺x | Ḻ | ¹
x | ⁺x | ¹x | ⁺x | ¹x | Ḻ | ¹ ∧	x | ⁺x | ⁺x | ⁺x | ⁺x | Ḻ | ¹ ∧
|[⁺]x | ⁺x | ⁺x | ¹x | Ḻ | λ	| ⁺x | ⁺x | ⁺x | Ḻ | Ḻ | ⁺
| Ḻ | Ḻ | Ḻ | λ	| Ḻ | Ḻ | Ḻ
| ⁺x | ¹x | ⁺x | ¹x | Ḻ | ¹	| ⁺x | ⁺x | ⁺x | ⁺x | Ḻ | ¹ ∧
x | ⁺x | ¹x | ⁺x | x́x ∧	| Ḻ | Ḻ x | ⁺x | Ḻ | ⁺ | ⁺x

Of the two rhythmical interpretations, that of Taylor is far preferable, because it follows the manuscript much more closely. I cannot agree, however, with Taylor's use of paused beats. In two strophes, enjambment connects the third line with fourth; in five others, the fourth and fifth lines are so connected. Although this does not prove that paused beats were not present in the melody, I feel the extensive use of enjambment does make the presence of such beats doubtful.

Kur interprets Taylor's *semibreves* and *minimae* as *breves* and *longae*, respectively, in the notation of this song in his review of Gennrich's Neidhart edition. The note with *cauda* which Taylor and Genn-

---

[14] Note that there is no indication of mode or measure. I should assume that there was a certain regularity, but here we should have, in the absence of music, no way of knowing whether the poem was written according to a melody in the first mode, in the second, or in neither. The melody could have even been in 2/4 time. In the first poem discussed, the linguistic material provided us with more information. The italicized *x* indicates occasional *Hebungsspaltung* (two short syllables for a long one). The dot represents occasional elision. If I had assumed double-stressed cadence, I should have schematized it as ⁺ x̣.

rich interpret as *minima* is usually used as *longa*; that without, as *brevis*.
Now we have a melody in the second mode, with a rhythmic pattern as
follows.

$$(\text{-}) \mid \acute{x} \text{-} \mid \acute{x} \text{-} \mid \acute{x} \text{-} \mid \acute{x} \text{-} \mid \acute{x} \, x$$
$$\text{-} \mid \acute{x} \text{-} \mid \acute{x} \text{-} \mid \acute{x} \text{-} \mid \acute{x} \text{-} \mid \acute{x} \, x$$
$$(\text{-}) [\mid \acute{x}\text{-}] \mid \acute{x} \text{-} \mid \acute{x} \text{-} \mid \acute{x} \text{-} \mid \acute{x} \, {\scriptstyle\wedge}$$
$$\mid \acute{x}xx \mid \acute{x} \, {\scriptstyle\wedge}$$
$$\mid \acute{x} \text{-} \mid \acute{x} \text{-} \mid \acute{x} \text{-} \mid \acute{x} \text{-} \mid \acute{x} \, x \text{-} \mid \acute{x} \text{-} \mid \acute{x} \text{-} \mid \acute{x} \text{-} \mid \acute{x} \, \text{.}^{15}$$

Between many of the lines we find an extension of the measure similar
to that Bertau has noted for some *Leiche,* for example, *sahen: end* =
$\mid \acute{x} \, x : \text{-} \mid$. If I had applied guideline (a) or (b) (see above) in making
my original schematization, I should have postulated double-stressed
cadence rather than feminine in these cases. I feel, however, that
double-stressed cadence should be used primarily to create four-beat
lines or half lines. In any case, if we accept the scansion in the second
mode, we do not have a double-stressed cadence.

Although Taylor is correct in pointing out that most metrical stresses
fall on long syllables (so also Bertau), this does not rule out the second
mode altogether. In this poem there are a few short stressed syllables
in addition to those split and those in the fourth lines, namely, I 1 *ligen,*
6 *sumer;* II 3 *sumer-;* III 1 *wisen,* 3 *sumer;* IV 1 *vogele;* V 1 *wider;*
VI 3 *ensulen,* 5 *schaden.* These should actually fit the second mode
better, since it would seem easier to stretch the unstressed syllables than
these stressed ones. Admittedly, this is a moot point. A stronger argument in favor of the last scansion is the treatment of the fourth line.
The words III *über al,* VII *der enkan,* IX *über al* can scarcely have been

---

¹⁵ The melody for the third line is one measure shorter than the text of the
critical edition (not one note, as Taylor states). Jammers, who agrees with
Taylor about the meaning of the note with *cauda* but whose transcription of
the melody is otherwise virtually identical with Kur's, lets the note over the
anacrusis serve for the whole first measure of the line. The fourth line generally
would be $\mid \acute{x} \text{-} \mid \acute{x}$ ($\mid \acute{x} x \mid \acute{x}$, if the manuscript is followed exactly) instead of
$\mid \acute{x}xx \mid \acute{x}$. The first line of the original probably sometimes had anacrusis, the
note for which is transmitted. Gennrich retains it as the first stressed note.
Taylor drops it. The anacrusis of the second and third line is not always present.

distorted as Taylor and Gennrich suggest.[16] If Neidhart had heard such an extended transitional melodic rhythm, surely the text would reflect it linguistically. The distortion of the linguistic material in the third and last lines which Gennrich proposes is also hardly possible. Readings like *díu bèide* must be rejected. Such distortions occasionally occur, but there is no reason to introduce them arbitrarily.

The key words in this sketch have been "it seems," "appears," "can be assumed," and the like. This does not mean that we know nothing, but rather that no two people know the same thing. What we cannot do, however, is to give up the search for answers; nor can we refuse to weigh the alternatives and discard our prejudices when we make our search. We must be critical, not only of theories and hypotheses, of assumptions and apparent facts, but also of our criticisms themselves.

[16] One possible way to read these lines with Taylor and Gennrich is to assume ornamentation which was not transmitted.

SELECTED BIBLIOGRAPHY

This list contains primarily studies the results of which are discussed in this sketch. For studies before 1961, refer also to *Der deutsche Minnesang: Aufsätze zu seiner Erforschung,* ed. Hans Fromm (Darmstadt, 1961), especially the literature cited in Wolfgang Mohr, "Zur Form des mittelalterlichen deutschen Strophenliedes: Fragen und Aufgaben," pp. 229–254, and Ursula Aarburg, "Melodien zum frühen deutschen Minnesang: Eine kritische Bestandaufnahme," pp. 378–421. See also the various volumes of the *Sammlung Metzler* and the bibliographical references in the works cited below.

GENERAL

Heusler, Andreas. *Deutsche Versgeschichte,* II. Berlin, 1927.

Mohr, Wolfgang. "Kadenz," *RL* (2nd ed.), I, 803–806. Berlin, 1955.

Paul, Otto, and Glier, Ingeborg. *Deutsche Metrik.* München, 1961. (Rev. Wolfgang Mohr, *AfdA* 76 [1965]: 145–153).

Jammers, Ewald. "Grundbegriffe der altdeutschen Versordnung." *ZfdA* 92 (1963): 241–248.

Taylor, Ronald J. "Minnesang—Wort und Wîse," *Essays in German Literature,* I, 1–28. London, 1965.

THEORY OF MODAL RHYTHMS

Kippenberg, Burkhard. *Der Rhythmus im Minnesang. Eine Kritik der literar- und musikhistorischen Forschung mit einer Übersicht über die musikalischen Quellen.* Munich, 1962. (Rev. Karl H. Bertau, *AfdA* 77 [1966]: 32–38).

Bertau, Karl Heinrich. *Sangverslyrik. Über Gestalt und Geschichtlichkeit mittelhochdeutscher Lyrik am Beispiel des Leichs.* Göttingen, 1964. (Rev. R. J. Taylor, *GGA* 218 [1966]: 114–118; Ewald Jammers, *PBB* 88 [1966]: 204–208; Werner Schröder, *ZfdPh* 84 [1965]: 625–637; Helmut Lomnitzer, *AfdA* 78 [1967]: 119–125; Hubert Heinen, *MLN,* 83 [1968]: 474–477).

Taylor, Ronald J. "Zur Übertragung der Melodien der Minnesänger." *ZfdA* 87 (1956–1957): 132–147.

Brunner, Wilhelm-Horst. "Walthers von der Vogelweide Palästinalied als Kontrafaktur." *ZfdA* 92 (1963): 195–211.

THEORY OF LONG LINES

Maurer, Friedrich. *Die religiösen Dichtungen des 11. und 12. Jahrhunderts,*
I, II. Tübingen, 1964. (Rev. Heinz Rupp, *ZfdPh* 85 [1966]: 450–458).

Beyschlag, Siegfried. "Langzeilen-Melodien." *ZfdA* 93 (1964): 157–176.

Schröder, Werner. "Zu alten unde neuen Theorien einer altdeutschen 'bin-
nengereimten Langzeile'." *PBB* 87 (1965): 150–165.

Schröder, Werner. "Versuch zu metrischer Beschreibung eines frühmittelhochdeutschen Gedichts mit einer forschungsgeschichtlichen Vorbemer-
kung. *ZfdA* 94 (1965): 196–213, 244–267.

STROPHIC STRUCTURE

Plenio, Kurt. "Beobachtungen zu Wolframs Liedstrophik." *PBB* 41 (1916):
47–127.

———. "Bausteine zur altdeutschen Strophik." *PBB* 42 (1917): 410–502;
PBB, 43 (1918): 56–99.

Hatto, A. T., and R. J. Taylor, "Recent Work on the Arithmetical Principle
in Medieval Poetry." *MLR* 46 (1951): 396–403.

Kuhn, Hugo. *Minnesangs Wende.* Tübingen, 1952, rev. ed. 1967.

Schirmer, Karl-Heinz. *Die Strophik Walthers von der Vogelweide. Ein
Beitrag zu den Aufbauprinzipien in der lyrischen Dichtung des Hochmittelalters.* Halle, 1956.

MUSIC EDITIONS

Jammers, Ewald. *Ausgewählte Melodien des Minnesangs.* Tübingen, 1963.

Taylor, Ronald J. *Die Melodien der weltlichen Lieder des Mittelalters*, I, II.
Stuttgart, 1964.

Hatto, A. T., and Taylor, R. J. *The Songs of Neidhart von Reuenthal.*
Manchester, 1958. (Rev. Karl H. Bertau, *AfdA* 72 [1960]: 23–35).

Rohloff, Ernst, *Neidharts Sangweisen*, I, II. Berlin, 1962. (Rev. Friedrich
Kur, *AfdA* 77 [1966]: 63–67).

Gennrich, Friedrich. *Neidhartlieder. Kritische Ausgabe der Neidhart von
Reuenthal zugeschriebenen Melodien.* Langen bei Frankfurt, 1962. (Rev.
Fr. Kur, *AfdA* 77 [1966]: 68–73).

numerical structure in medieval literature

BY MICHAEL S. BATTS

But thou hast ordered all things in measure, and number, and weight[1]

Look at the sky and the earth and the sea, and whatever shines brightly above or creeps below or flies or swims. They have forms because they have numbers. Take these away, and nothing will be left.[2]

Since number is therefore something of greatest universality, it rightly belongs to metaphysics, if you take metaphysics to be the science of those properties which are common to all classes of beings.[3]

n o one will, I think, wish to gainsay that we are all to a greater or lesser extent imbued with a belief in the significance if not the beauty of numbers. The quotations with which I have prefaced this paper are intended to substantiate the existence of this feeling. But in discussing numbers in connection with literature, in looking at literature through the eyes of an arithmetician as it were, if not a computer, one seems to offend against an unspoken tabu. This is due in large measure, I suppose, to our having been conditioned since the Romantics to viewing the process of poetic creation as divinely inspired but somehow unplanned and therefore unorganized. Consequently we find it difficult to accept either the work of critics who seek to approach the meaning of medieval works through a study of the arithmetical form, or, for that matter, of modern poets who seek new forms of expression

---

[1] Wisdom 11: 21.

[2] St. Augustine, *De libero arbitrio*, II, 42.

[3] Leibniz, *De Arte Combinatoria*, III, 7.

and seek to express new forms of experience in a way which seems calculated and mechanical, and therefore unpoetic.[4]

Involved also is probably our innate aversion to the reduction to a
mere digit, a cipher, either of ourselves or of a work of human creative
endeavor. To put it in simple language, we object to being reduced to
a number of small holes—square ones at that—in an IBM card. Although the computer may thereby match the coded characteristics of
marriage candidates more satisfactorily than the fortuneteller using the
hallowed tradition of gematria—matching the numerical values of the
persons' names—the aversion remains, and it infuses our attitude toward the analysis of a work of art on the basis of machine-scanned
mathematical symbols.

In a way it is not surprising that this objection should be so strong,
for, although numbers play an ever-increasing role in our lives, they
have with a few exceptions almost entirely lost any deeper significance.
They have become as it were secularized; and although a work of cubist
art or even a modern novel may still have a numerical pattern as its
basis, the pattern is an abstraction rather than a religious or philosophi-
cally meaningful order.[5]

This was not so in the medieval period and even much later, when
numbers and numerical relationships were considered fundamental evidence of the omnipresence of divine order, of the Great Mathematician, and rather than attempting to gain control over the universe and
render it a chaos, as it now seems to do, scientific endeavor was then
directed to uncovering the planned harmony of the universe; this harmony itself was poetry, was music, the music to which Shakespeare
refers when Lorenzo says of the night sky: "There's not the smallest
orb which thou behold'st/But in his motion like an angel sings."[6]

---

[4] The "mechanical" approach is not necessarily new. Compare, for example,
Leibniz' suggestion for finding new modes of poetic expression in his *De arte
combinatoria*, discussed by E. Reed in "Leibniz, Wieland and the Combinatory
Principle," *MLR* 56 (1961) 529–537.

[5] Thomas Mann's *Der Zauberberg* is perhaps the most obvious example of
the use of "symbolic" numbers. For an example of numerically structured
novels, compare Gerd Gaiser's *Sterbende Jagd* and *Schlußball*.

[6] *The Merchant of Venice,* Act V, sc. 1; cf. the remark by Joseph Hauer:

Since this view was common to the whole of Christendom, since this Christendom was still very much of a cultural unity, but since also this culture felt itself to be the direct continuation of classical tradition (just as imperial power had been transferred to the Holy Roman Empire), I shall refer in this essay also to works outside the period with which we are mainly concerned, and in languages other than German. Because of the limited space, my remarks must in any case be discursive: rather than attempt to offer new material or new interpretations of familiar works, I shall review the work recently done in the field of numerical composition with a view to pointing to major problems and questions, the discussion of which should prove interesting and valuable. If my examples are mainly drawn from narrative poetry, it is not only because my work has been done almost exclusively in this field, but because I also wish to open the question of the relationship between the structural concepts of narrative and lyrical poetry. But above all I must stress that I shall not discuss the merits of the numerical patterns proposed by various critics, since whether or not I agree with their views is not material to the question at large.

First, I would like to sketch as briefly as possible the development of studies of what is now commonly known as numerical composition—*Zahlenkomposition*. The subject is in a way not new; we are all familiar, for example, with Lachmann's predilection for numerical patterns, but the two important starting points are works by Max Ittenbach in 1937[7] and E. R. Curtius in 1948. The former concerned himself exclusively with German works of the period of the Salian emperors; the latter offered in the fifteenth excursus of his *Europäische Literatur und lateinisches Mittelalter*[8] a considerable number of examples of works deliberately planned to have a length—that is to say, a number of lines, stanzas, and so forth—that was in some way or other meaningful numerically. Interest in such matters must have been in the air, however,

---

"Meine Zwölftonmusik ist die Sprache des Universums, die Offenbarung der Weltordnung, die Harmonie der Sphären" (quoted from *Der Spiegel* no. 22 (1966), p. 116.

[7] Max Ittenbach, *Deutsche Dichtungen der salischen Kaiserzeit und verwandte Denkmäler* (Würzburg: Triltsch, 1937).

[8] (4th ed.; Bern/Munich: Francke, 1963 [1948]).

for at about the same time and in the following years, studies appeared on numerical composition in the vernacular literatures of Western Europe from Iceland to Italy—sometimes apparently without the author's being aware of the work done elsewhere. This is significant for two reasons: although it shows, first, the independence of the work done, it also reveals the regrettable isolation in which scholars in specialized fields tend to work. For example, in his book on Spenser published in 1960, A. K. Hieatt[9] does not mention a similar discovery by Le Grelle in Virgil's *Georgics*, published in 1949;[10] Eggers' article on the *Ludwigslied,* published also in 1960,[11] mentions neither Le Grelle's work nor Huismann's analysis of the *Ludwigslied*, published in 1950.[12] It is clear that what is required at present is the pursuit of such studies on a comparative basis, for only in this way will it be possible to come to valid conclusions as to the nature, extent, and transmission of ideas.

What, then, are these numbers and what are the numerical patterns with which scholars have become in some cases so passionately involved (and I use the word "involved" deliberately)? All readers of medieval literature are accustomed to meeting certain numbers with great frequency, numbers which even today may still have a certain significance —7, 12, and 40 are perhaps the prime examples. Although there may be some signs of individuality—the *Nibelungenlied,*[13] for example, chooses numbers of no real significance—these and other numbers, which are familiar from the Christian and the native tradition and as such are hallowed by centuries of use, occur over and over again. They have been variously designated, one of the most frequently used terms being "typische Zahlen."

[9] A. K. Hieatt, *Short Time's Endless Monument. The Symbolism of the Numbers in Edmund Spenser's Epithalamion* (New York: Columbia University Press, 1960).

[10] G. Le Grelle, "Le premier livre des Géorgiques, poème pythagoricien," *Études classiques* 17 (1949), 139–235.

[11] H. Eggers, "Der goldene Schnitt im Aufbau alt- und mittelhochdeutscher Epen," *Wirkendes Wort* 10 (1960), 193–203.

[12] J. A. Huismann, *Neue Wege zur dichterischen und musikalischen Technik Walthers von der Vogelweide* (Utrecht: Kemink en zoon, 1950).

[13] Cf. B. Q. Morgan, "On the Use of Numbers in the *Nibelungenlied*," *JEGP* 36 (1937), 10–20.

Although these numbers, scattered through the pages of every medieval work, have no relation to structure, which is our immediate concern, the total work itself—that is, the number of lines, stanzas, chapters, or books—may also evidence a number remarkable either for its meaning or simply for its aesthetic quality, its "roundness." Round numbers are of course the decades or, in a duodecimal system, perhaps also the 12 and its multiples, and these numbers may also be meaningful in their context; but usually much more significant are such numbers as 17, 22, 34. Many such examples (mostly from the Romance languages) may be found in the essay by Curtius, and for this aspect of numerical composition Tschirch has coined the phrase "symbolbestimmter Umfang."[14]

But this again is "merely" the total of lines, stanzas, and so on. Even more interesting are works where the subdivisions, first into chapters and then into stanza or line groups of smaller and smaller size, are either symmetrical and aesthetically pleasing or significant in relation to the subject matter. A simple example of the latter is Otfried's *Evangelienharmonie*, with its division into 5 books for the 5 human senses; the chapters total 5 times 28 (140)—or, with the dedications, 144. The late Middle English *Pearl* contains 101 stanzas, 1,212 lines. Dante's *Divine Comedy* is well known to have 3 times 33 plus 1 cantos, to make up the perfect 100. The *Ackermann aus Böhmen* has 34 chapters, and the final prayer, 7 paragraphs. Complications may arise when the total number is significant, such as the 49 of the stanzas of the *Annolied*, but where the work is *not* divided into 7 groups of 7, just as Otfried's work is *not* divided into 5 books of exactly 28 chapters each.

As for the division of a secular work into balanced groups of lines or stanzas, this is normally a question of symmetry. Although the structure may reflect the relative importance of details of the narrative—may, through the pattern, connect separated but related portions of the narrative—the numbers themselves remain without meaning either per se or in the context: they express what Eggers has described as the *Sym-*

[14] F. Tschirch, "Zum symbolbestimmten Umfang mittelalterlicher Dichtungen." In *Stil- und Formprobleme in der Literatur* (Vorträge beim VII. Kongress d. Int. Ver. f. mod. Sp. u. Lit. in Heidelberg) (Heidelberg: Carl Winter, 1959).

metrie und Proportion epischen Erzählens.[15] Kienast has given numerous examples from Wolfram's *Willehalm*;[16] he posits, for example, in the death scene of Vivian, the following line groups: 16-46-28-46-16. In Gottfried's *Tristan* the introduction and description of the dog Petitcreiu takes up precisely 100 lines,[17] which has presumably no significance at all. Borderline difficulties may of course be produced by the smaller numbers which are intrinsically significant. For example, Wolfram's *Parzival* is (probably) made up of 16 books; the religious climax is the ninth book. Is this significant or merely an example of symmetrical structure?

I can neither list here the many types of structure nor give examples of them all. It is also not my intention, as I said before, to enter into a discussion of the validity of the individual theories that have been put forward. Frequently the forms in secular works depend upon some kind of symmetrical layout, the most common being repetition—ABC/ABC—a mirror pattern ABC/CBA—or a recess pattern—ABCBA. The number of elements and relative length are of course variable. The nature of these patterns, however, and the type of numerical reference cannot fully be appreciated without some examples, and I shall therefore offer an indication of the numerical correspondences in three works from widely separated periods and cultures, part of my aim being to demonstrate the diffusion and persistence of the tradition.

Omitting the introductory 4.5 lines, the first book of the *Georgics* may be viewed[18] as consisting of groups of 37.5, 161. 55, 204.5, and 51.5 lines, an apparently asymmetrical though roughly balanced sequence. However, the total of the second and fourth groups is 365.5, or the number of days in a year; the total of the first, third, and fifth groups is 144, or the square of the number of months in the year. Furthermore, this number 144 is made up of an inner group of 55 and

[15] The title of a monograph on Hartmann von Aue (Stuttgart: Klett, 1956).

[16] R. Kienast, "Zur Tektonik von Wolframs Willehalm," *Studien zur deutschen Philologie* (Festschrift Friedrich Panzer) (Heidelberg: Carl Winter, 1950), 96–115.

[17] *Tristan und Isolde,* ed. F. Ranke (Berlin and Frankfurt/Main: Weidmann, 1949), ll. 15791–15890.

[18] Le Grelle, "Le premier livre des Géorgiques," p. 149.

other groups totaling 89—which is the exact division of 144 by the Golden Section.

The *Annolied* has been subjected to so much numerical interpretation that I am loath to use it as an example,[19] but I shall restrict myself to broad outlines. It is clear that the total number of stanzas, 49, is significant as 7 times 7. The major divisions are after the 7th and 33rd stanzas, at which latter point we are told that Anno is the 33rd bishop and that 7 of his predecessors have been canonized. The actual life of Anno is related in the final 16 stanzas, another square number and one half of the length of the preceding portion, omitting the introductory stanza. Eggers[20] finds that the strange total of 878 verse lines (the stanzas are of irregular length) shows evidence of the golden mean, for the sum of the lines of the introductory stanza and the 16 stanzas on Anno himself is 336 (1–18 and 561–878) against 542 (19–560) for the "Weltgeschichte."

In his book on Spenser's *Epithalamion*[21] A. K. Hieatt finds that the division of the poem into 24 stanzas represents the hours of the day (the stanzas, like those of the *Annolied,* are of irregular form), but despite the thematic and linguistic association of stanza 1 with 13, 2 with 14, and so forth, the passage from day to night actually takes place part way through stanza 17. This points to the proportionate length of day and night on that day and for that part of the world where the marriage is celebrated. The long lines of the poem number 365, which is straightforward enough. However, these long lines are distributed in a curious manner, 15 or 16 per stanza with 6 separated off in a so-called envoy. This is apparently done to draw the fine distinction between the solar and the sidereal motion. Each day the sun moves through one degree less in its orbit than the fixed stars—that is to say, through only 359 degrees. In this way it drops back relative to the fixed stars 1 hour every 15 or 16 days, returning to its original position after 365 days.

These brief examples may give some idea of the extent and motivation of such numerical correspondences, though I must add that the details I have given are far from complete and one could cite more com-

[19] See Bibliography.
[20] Eggers, "Der goldene Schnitt," p. 200.
[21] See note 9.

plex or more esoteric examples. In case I should be accused of repeat-
ing the fantastic inventions of experts in numerological sleight of
hand, let me hasten to quote from a skeptic in this field who involved
himself in some highly complicated numerical correspondences in the
Evangelienharmonie and cried out for a mathematician to demonstrate
to him that such correspondences could be gratuitous: "Vielleicht kann
mir jemand beweisen, dass alles Unsinn ist; ich wäre gar nicht betrübt,
wäre dann meine alte Skepsis doch wieder berechtigt."[22]

Looking dispassionately, there would seem to be overwhelming evidence for the existence of numerical structural patterns and of highly
involved play on numbers in various cultures throughout the Middle
Ages, perhaps the strangest thing about the whole problem being the
complete lack of any contemporary references to such practices. A few
years ago I made the attempt to demonstrate that the religious and the
secular forms derive on the one hand from Christian numerical exegesis
and on the other from classical secular sources, but that both derive
ultimately from neo-Pythagorean number mysticism. Future research
may well not bear out this suggestion; in particular it may be possible to
establish direct connection between classical sources and the later Middle Ages or Renaissance, but for the time being we must bear in mind
that the two traditions do exist. Although the clerical writers refer not
infrequently to their source for the numerical interpretation, the secular
writers, despite their often quoted insistence on naming the source of
their material, are (unlike modern authors) totally silent about their
workshop practices. Karl-Heinz Schirmer in his work on Walther von

---

[22] Heinz Rupp, "Otfried von Weissenburg und die Zahlen," *Archiv* 201
(1964/1965), 262–265, esp. p. 265. On checking this work myself, I did indeed
find that much of the symmetry derives from the curious characteristics of
multiples of 3, in particular the fact that the *Quersumme* of any multiple of 3 is
alternately 3, 6, or 9 and that no matter how any such number is divided up,
the *Quersumme* of the smaller numbers will always be the same as that of the
total. Professor Rupp subsequently wrote to me in this connection: ". . . ich bin
heute durchaus nicht mehr sicher, daß diese ganzen Zahlendinge immer auf
Symbolzahlen und Planung der Autoren zurückzuführen sind." The question of
whether the authors were themselves aware of such mathematical peculiarities
remains (at least pro tempore) unanswerable.

der Vogelweide[23] makes much of Ulrich von Strasburg's *Summa de bono*,[24] but though this author may be more discursive than most about the laws of beauty, his primary concern—the question of the essence of beauty in a Christian sense, its emanation from the good, its relation to evil, and so on—is religious, and in consequence the work offers us in fact little more than do the medieval *Artes*. The *Artes* themselves, of course, are not concerned at all with the technical division of the material, but chiefly with the method of embellishing it. The only clear reference to so-called workshop practice appears to be Bishop Hincmar's *Explanatio in ferculum Salomonis*.[25] Curiously enough the original work is lost, although the detailed explanation of the reasons for the number of lines has been preserved.

Summing up, however, it would seem impossible for similar practices to have been employed in Augustan Rome, post-Carolingian Germany, medieval Iceland, and Renaissance England without there being some form of tradition and thus, by implication, of transmission.

To go one stage further toward the *Minnesang*, it is equally unlikely, especially in view of the close relationship between music and mathematics, that in as highly sophisticated and consciously restrictive a form of "literary art" as *Minnesang*, such popular practices were avoided. Naturally enough, one would not expect to find the complex patterns and ramified relationships that are to be found in lengthier epics and other narrative works, and perhaps it would be better altogether if one were able to approach the *Minnesang* without previous knowledge of what has been done in other fields, but the damage has now been done: inevitably one has recollections of other studies. One must then ask: is there also evidence of such numerical composition in *Minnesang*?

The simplest example from Walther's work is probably the *Lied*

---

[23] K.-H. Schirmer, *Die Strophik Walthers von der Vogelweide. Ein Beitrag zu den Aufbauprinzipien in der lyrischen Dichtung des Hochmittelalters* (Halle/Saale: VEB Max Niemeyer, 1956).

[24] Ulrich Engelbert von Straßburg, *Summa de bono,* ed. M. Grabmann *MSB* 1925, 5 (Munich, 1926).

[25] Migne *PL* Vol. 125, col. 817–834.

beginning "Minne diu hat einen site" (57,23),[26] of which lines 7 and 8 read:

> Ir sint vier unt zwenzec jar
> vil lieber danne ir vierzec sin,—

a simple description of youth preferred over age, but underlined by the form of the poem, which has 40 lines, 40 feet in each stanza, and 24 feet in each *Aufgesang* (I use the term "foot" for the German *Takt* rather than the musical term "bar").[27]

The most famous of Walther's *Sprüche*, "Ich saz uf eime steine" (8,4), has 25 four-foot lines, making a satisfying round total of 100.

In the "Elegie" as Maurer calls it—"Ouwe war sint verswunden alliu miniu jar" (124,1)—there are 3 stanzas, each of 33 half lines. Each stanza has in each half line 3 feet, with the exception of the penultimate, which has 4, so that each stanza has in effect 3 times 33 plus 1, or 100 feet. The whole poem thus has 300 feet, a number represented by the Greek letter T, the symbol of the cross, an association which would fit in with the content of the closing lines.[28]

In the *Palästinalied* (14,38) we find a kind of numerical association not unusual in religious works. There are (probably) 7 stanzas of 7 lines each. Each stanza has 28 feet, the number associated with the Virgin Mary. Christ is first mentioned in the 7th line, Mary in the 12th (she is traditionally supposed to have borne Christ at the age of 12), and Christ's Resurrection figures in line 34, about which no comment is necessary.[29]

Thus in these poems we find evidence of a purely playful use of number; of a round number, possibly with significance (100); and of the use of numbers with a numerical religious association appropriate to

[26] Quotations are from the edition by Friedrich Maurer, *1 Die religiösen und die politischen Lieder* (Tübingen: Niemeyer Verlag, 1955), and *2 Die Liebeslieder* (Tübingen: Niemeyer Verlag, 1956).

[27] Huismann, *Neue Wege,* p. 51; Schirmer, *Die Strophik,* p. 89.

[28] Huismann, *Neue Wege, passim,* especially pp. 47–51.

[29] Schirmer, *Die Strophik,* pp. 113–115. Cf. also Schupp (Bibliography, no. 72) which was not available to me at the time of writing.

the context. For a vastly more complex set of associations I refer you to Huismann's analysis of the *Marienleich* (3,1).[30]

Walter Schirmer has analyzed Walther's *Lieder* at some length in his work on the stanza form, and I shall restrict myself in the following to a discussion of the points he makes—not, however, from a metrical-technical but only from a numerotechnical point of view.

Basically he makes the following claims (p. 149 f.):

(a) There is a correspondence between the parts of the poem, "eine theoretisch-abstrakte, in der Zahl ausgedrückte Abstimmung der Glieder," Ulrich's *consonantia partium inter se*.

(b) There is a correspondence between the stanza length in feet and the poem as a whole, that is, the number of lines, a "Wechselbeziehung in den Grössenverhältnissen von Strophe und Lied . . . von einer abstrakten, mit verschiedenen Masswerten: Takt und Verse berechneten theoretischen *consonantia partium in relatione ad totum corpus* hergestellt."

(c) The numbers are deliberately chosen from those with significance, "charakteristische Zahlen."[31]

I find Schirmer's analyses of the individual *Lieder* convincing on the whole. I would agree first of all that there is a not unnatural desire on the part of the poet to achieve a harmonious balance between the parts of the stanza, a harmony expressible numerically. As for planning the stanza to have the same number of feet as the whole work has lines, I am not greatly impressed, since by Schirmer's own evidence this "rule" obtains in only one out of every five poems—not a very high proportion.

With his definition of "charakteristische Zahlen," and with his use of them, I am far from satisfied, for if we look at the totals given in tabular form for the number of feet per stanza, we find the following numbers: 20, 28, 32, 34, 35, 36, 40, 44, 48, 52, 56, 58, 64, 68, 80, 100. Of these only 28, 34, and 68 can definitely be claimed as signifi-

---

[30] Huismann, *Neue Wege*, pp. 53–57.

[31] These are what I earlier called "typische Zahlen"; Schirmer's explanation is: "Durch häufigen Gebrauch haben die Symbolzahlen . . . weithin ihren symbolischen Wert verloren und sind zu bloßen Kompositionszahlen geworden."

cant; 36 and 40 might be added. On the other hand the—to Schirmer natural—Germanic propensity to compose in a four-beat line would lead naturally to multiples of 4 and in fact we find every multiple of 4 from 20 to 68, with the exception of 24 and 60. One would also expect a heavy concentration around the middle of the scale, and if we extract the poems with numbers between 32 and 40, we find they account for 45, or over half the total. I am not anxious to attack the problem so statistically, but it must be pointed out that the spread of numbers is almost entirely consonant with a natural spread of length; there is almost no evidence of preferred numbers.

Not that Schirmer himself is without a preference for specific numbers, as is evidenced by his discussion of the *Rügeton*—"Selbwahsen kint du bist ze krump" (101,23)—which will provide us with an introduction to the last part of my essay, a consideration of the methodology of numerical analysis.

In discussing this *Lied* Schirmer takes Hatto to task for finding 70 feet in the stanza,[32] since—in Hatto's own words: "This [that is, 68] is a wretched number . . . . Acceptance of 70 with the above subdivisions relieves metricists of all need to dispute whether the feminine rhymes in the fourth pes are heavy or light; *numbers demand* that it be 3 bars long and therefore light . . . ."[33] Schirmer objects here to the priority given to the number and concludes his objection with the claim: "Damit wären der Wilkür des Bearbeiters Tor und Tür geöffnet" (p. 137). But Schirmer himself, in discussing "Ich han ir so wol gesprochen" (40,19), writes: "Unterstützt von der Beobachtung, dass die Potenzzahl $6^2 = 36$ als Kompositionszahl für den Gesamtumfang einer Strophe bei Walther ungewöhnlich häufig begegnet [14 times], wird man sich auch *aus zahlenkompositorischen Gründen* dazu entschliessen, nach dem 1. Abgesangsvers eine Pause anzusetzen" (p. 42, my italics); and on the *Lied* "Staet ist angest unde not" (96,29) he writes: "Da der Aufgesang 24 Takte zählt, der Abgesang aber nur 22 ausgefüllte Takte umfasst, muss tatsächlich mit zwei gewerteten

[32] Schirmer, *Die Strophik,* pp. 136–139.
[33] A. T. Hatto, "On Beauty of Numbers in Wolfram's Dawn Songs (An Improved Metrical Canon)," *MLR* 45 (1950), 180–188. The quotation is p. 182, the italics mine.

Pausen im Abgesang gerechnet werden, *zumal es eine Gesamttaktzahl 46 bei Walther sonst nicht gibt"* (p. 49, my italics).

Our concern is not the relative significance of 68 or 70—both of which numbers have, I would say, about equal symbolic value, the 70 occurring quite frequently and the 68 being important only as twice 34—but the principle involved: how does one arrive at an objective estimation of the numerical composition of any given work? What criteria are there for elucidating these patterns?

There are to my mind only two possible types of objective criteria for the elucidation of numerical composition. The first of these is textual, the second, illustrative. Under textual evidence I would include not only such straightforward statements as Otfried's explanation of the reason for dividing his work into five books, but also oblique references and guarded indications, what Tschirch has called "versteckte Schlüsselzahlen."[34] Examples of these are the poem of Walther quoted above (on 24 and 40) or the commencement of the last group of lines in the analysis of the *Georgics* with the phrase "sol tibi signum dabit" —the total, you will recall, being 144. A more complex example is provided by the opening lines of the *Heliand,* where the relationship between the Trinity and the Gospels, between the 3 and 4, is stressed.[35] The numeral 4 occurs first in line 9 (3×3), then in line 16 (4×4), and then in line 32 ($16 + 16$). In lines 10–12 the 3 (or 4?) gifts from heaven—actually the Trinity with two synonymous terms for the Holy Spirit—are described: $3 \times 4 = 12$. In addition to such numbers there is of course one other form of textual evidence, namely stylistic devices. Rathofer makes much of this in his study of the *Heliand,* lines 9 and 16, for example, the lines in which the numeral 4 occurs, have almost identical first half lines:

> frummian, firiho barn . . . (9)
> firiho barno frummian   (16)

[34] Fritz Tschirch, "Schlüsselzahlen. Studie zur geistigen Durchdringung der Form in der deutschen Dichtung des Mittelalters." In *Beiträge zur deutschen und nordischen Literatur* (Festgabe für Leopold Magon) (Berlin: Akademie Verlag, 1958).

[35] The following after J. Rathofer, *Der Heliand. Theologischer Sinn als tektonische Form* (Cologne/Graz: Böhlau, 1962).

More familiar perhaps is Gottfried's use of echoing phrases marking the beginning and end of line groups.

By the second type of evidence, which I have termed illustrative, I mean manuscript indications of structure. Under this category may be included not merely such obvious things as titles and subtitles, but also rubrics, capital letters, illumination and even marginal signs. In the Heidelberg manuscript of *Tristan*, for example, the *Initialenspiel* has been well preserved, but more interesting, perhaps, is the fact that the beginning and the end of the passage on the dog Petitcreiu, the passage I cited earlier as having exactly 100 lines, are indicated by marginal signs, and similar signs are to be found elsewhere. It is true that succeeding generations of scribes may obliterate or obscure such manuscript indications, but where numerous manuscripts are available it is possible to reconstruct the original with some degree of accuracy.

At that point, I believe, the objective criteria are already exhausted. From here on, as Eggers says: "scheiden sich die Geister im literaturwissenschaftlichen Methodenstreit."[36] On the one hand there is the traditional approach, which would base structural analysis entirely upon content; on the other is the radical approach represented by Eggers, which would investigate the meaning of the work on the basis of the structure, which has been determined purely mathematically—"Im Vertrauen auf die gehaltbindende Transparenz der Form sind wir von *dieser* ausgegangen."[37]

This he writes at the conclusion of his essay on the *Ludwigslied* and it will be instructive to compare briefly four recent attempts to arrive at the structure of this work, in particular in view of the claim that has been advanced that the *Ludwigslied* is in fact a *Leich*. In order to facilitate discussion I shall quote not in chronological order but in order of similarity, and reduce all the divisions to half lines so that there is a common factor.[38]

---

[36] Eggers, "Der goldene Schnitt," p. 199.

[37] *Ibid.*

[38] Ittenbach, *Deutsche Dichtungen,* pp. 19–27; F. Willems, "Der parataktische Satzstil im *Ludwigslied,*" *ZfdA* 85 (1954), 18–35; Eggers, *Der goldene Schnitt;* Huismann, *Neue Wege.*

Ittenbach (1937):	16		24	12 8 22		26		10
Willems (1954):	16	8	16 12 8	22 8			18 10	
Eggers (1960):		24		36	22		36	
Huismann (1950):	16		16 16 22 16			16		16

Ittenbach bases himself entirely on the content, although he, too, claims that medieval poets constructed their works on the basis of meaningful numbers, just as in the case of the proportions of church buildings, and he adds: "Damit ist dann allerdings ein Ansatz gewonnen, der für die Interpretation der gesamten Dichtung einen festen Richtpunkt abgibt" (p. 3), which suggests at least that interpretation may be dependent on form. Willems follows Ittenbach to a large extent.

Huismann and Eggers, on the other hand, go different ways. Huismann works from the stanzas as units, reducing them first to numbers of half lines as suggested by the manuscript. There are not only points between the half lines in the manuscript, but also capital letters for the second half lines. Having written them out as groups of 4 or 6, he is able to find a symmetrical grouping, groups of 16 surrounding a central group of 22. This is done entirely without reference to content, something Eggers claims to do but in fact does not do. Eggers first assumes on the basis of content an introduction of 12 lines and separates this from the main body of the work (making three groups of 4 lines each), he then divides the main part into groups of 18, 11, and 18 lines on the basis of the fact that the king's speech forms a unit of 11 lines in the middle. This provides him with an example of the golden section, 11:18, and the sum of these two numbers provides the intervening number 29, in the series between 11, 18, 29, and 47, the last being of course the total number of lines in the main body of the poem. Only then does Eggers use this arithmetical consideration as a basis for interpretation. He posits as focal points the lines 27 and 45, these lines being the mid-point of the first and second, the second and third parts, respectively.

$$12(3 \times 4):11\text{-}18\text{-}11 = 47$$
$$29 \quad 29$$

Leaving aside the question of the merits of his interpretation, his premises at least are certainly not what he claims them to be, for, like Ittenbach and Willems before him, he uses the content as a basis for arriving at a first understanding of the form. Although he puts forward a radical viewpoint, he is not as true to it as Huismann, who totally ignores content and arrives at an unquestionably, even strikingly, simpler structure, but one which cuts across all content divisions.

Faced with these diverging results, one might tend to shrug off the whole question or, at most, accept the more attractive solution and dismiss the others as mere chimeras. But this would be fair neither to the modern critic nor to the medieval poet. There is no reason to assume that the poet was not capable of putting such complex mathematical correspondences into his work; on the contrary, there is good reason for him to do so. It is not for nothing that one of the most frequently quoted Biblical phrases was from the Book of Wisdom: "But thou hast ordered all things in measure, and number, and weight." Wisdom itself, Augustine claimed, was not only *in* number, it *was* number,[39]—"The fact, however, surely is that somehow they are one and the same thing"—and he goes on to say, "Yet, since Sacred Scripture says about wisdom that she reacheth from end to end mightily and ordereth all things sweetly, that power by which she reacheth from end to end mightily perhaps signifies number." Later he writes: "I do not suggest for a moment that wisdom is found lower when compared to number, since it is the same; but it demands an eye capable of discerning it."

The fact, then, that the numerical pattern is not at first evident, that it was and must have been hidden from the audience, or indeed from a reading public, does not weigh either against the belief in a structural pattern related to the work and content or against the possibility that a complex numerical pattern may have been built into the work independent of the content. This is in fact the crux of the problem. I did not previously include content in my suggestion for the objective criteria in establishing numerical patterns. This is because, in the first place, definition of content already depends in part on interpretation— and in particular the unclear distinction between *Gehalt* and *Inhalt*

---

[39] The following quotations from *De libero arbitrio*, II, 30 and 32.

renders such bases liable to much dispute—and, in the second place, the content itself may be in no way related to the numerical pattern. This, I think, is the lesson to be learned from the *Ludwigslied*: there may quite well be a formal metrical or musical—that is, arithmetical— pattern that runs counter to the apparent poetic structure, thus cutting across sense divisions. This is, I feel, an important principle, but before turning finally to the meaning in general of such practices, let me first discuss briefly the possible practical applications.

To my mind, the most fascinating aspect of this kind of work has been the frequency with which the manuscript text has, by a study of the form, been vindicated against the revisions of nineteenth-century authors, in whose hands texts have suffered almost as much as from the much-maligned medieval scribes. Schirmer's work gives us valuable pointers in this direction. Rathofer's study of the *Heliand* vindicates the MS. against the scholarly theory of interpolations. Duckworth's work on the *Aeneid*[40] demonstrates the validity of the mid-line divisions which some editors have seen fit to "correct." Such discoveries have, I feel, given new impetus and a new direction to manuscript studies.

In the case of *Minnesang* it would also be instructive to investigate the possibility of development in structural patterns in order to gain assistance in the task of assessing relative chronology. It is noteworthy that Schirmer suggests a "development" but does not specifically consider this aspect. For example, he entitles two sections of one chapter "Beginnende Lockerung . . ." and "Fortschreitende Lockerung. . . ." As far as I am aware, the only attempt in this direction has been made by Professor Hatto, who in the essay on Wolfram quoted above suggests a chronology on the basis of the structural patterns, actually on the basis of "a sequence of diminishing totals."

In narrative works we gain (from the point of view of interpretation) deeper insight into the meaning of the narrative—and I feel that we would do well to remember that, despite some modern critics,

---

[40] G. E. Duckworth, *Structural Patterns and Proportions in Vergil's Aeneid, a Study in Mathematical Composition* (Ann Arbor: University of Michigan Press, 1962).

there is a meaning in the narrative; parts of the plot, statements of characters, even descriptions, gain in significance if it is realized that they are linked not only stylistically but also by the compositional pattern.

But there is a deeper significance in these numerical patterns—in the medieval obsession with numbers, which cannot be understood except by reference to other forms of literature and art. Partaking of divine wisdom, numbers are woven into the fabric of literary works, just as below the literal meaning of a fable there is the allegorical and below this the symbolic level of meaning. In creating these intricate patterns it mattered to the medieval poet not at all that his subtleties of composition—if indeed they may be called that—would never be appreciated by the audience or reader, any more than it mattered to the stonemason that the details of his carving on the spire of a cathedral would never even be seen once the scaffolding was removed. The universe was a divinely ordered and inspired harmony, and the poet was concerned to put into his work some small part of this order. Only if we can turn our minds from admiration (or, of course, disapproval) of the complexity of such practices as those I have discussed and learn to appreciate the motives that inspired them, can we gain deeper insight into the mind of the creators of these works. Perhaps by so doing we may also recover in this disjointed time something of the lost feeling of the harmony of the universe.

BIBLIOGRAPHY

The number of works on number, number systems, and numerology is vast, and no attempt is made here to list works of a general nature or works on specific numbers. What follows is a fairly comprehensive list of works dealing with numerical composition in the broad sense of the term in Old and Middle High German literature. In the introductory section I have listed a few works of more general nature or works containing comprehensive references to numerical composition in related fields. The individual items are numbered and the literary works discussed are listed in alphabetical order.

GENERAL

1. Dunbar, H. F. *Symbolism in Medieval Thought and Its Consummation in the Divine Comedy.* New Haven: Yale University Press (London: Oxford University Press), 1929; New York: Russell & Russell, 1961.
2. Hopper, V. F. *Medieval Number Symbolism.* New York: Columbia University Press, 1938.
3. Sauer, Joseph. "Zahlensymbolik," *Lexikon für Theologie und Kirche* Vol. 10 Freiburg/Br.: Herder, 1938.
4. ———. *Symbolik des Kirchengebäudes und seiner Ausstattung in der Auffassung des Mittelalters (mit Berücksichtigung von Honorius Augustodunensis, Sicardus und Durandus.)* Freiburg/Br.: Herder, 1902; 2nd ed., 1924.
5. Großmann, Ursula. "Studien zur Zahlensymbolik des Frühmittelalters." *Zs. für kath. Theologie* 76 (1954): 19–54. On Augustinus, Hincmar, Alkuin, cf. her dissertation of the same title Freiburg/Br., 1948.
6. Knopf, Wilhelm. *Zur Geschichte der typischen Zahlen in der deutschen Litteratur des Mittelalters.* Ph.D. dissertation. Leipzig: Glausch, 1902. Very little use.
7. Curtius, Ernst Robert. *Europäische Literatur und lateinisches Mittelalter.* Bern/Munich: Francke [1948] 1963, 4th ed.: Exkurs XV, Zahlenkomposition pp. 491–498. Almost exclusively examples from Romance languages.
8. Batts, Michael S. "The Origins of Numerical Symbolism and Numerical Patterns in Medieval German Literature." *Traditio* 20 (1964): 462–471.
9. Lange, Wolfgang. "Zahlen und Zahlenkomposition in der *Edda.*"

Beitr. 77 (Halle, 1955): 306–348. Numerous references to further studies on numbers and/or form in the *Edda* and an excursus on numbers in *Beowulf*.

10. Robson, C. A. "The Techniques of Symmetrical Composition in Medieval Narrative Poetry," *Studies in Medieval French presented to Alfred Ewert* (Oxford: Clarendon, 1961), 26–75. With discussion of *Yvain*, Sir Launfal, and Tristan (Beroul and Eilhart).

11. Duckworth, G. E. *Structural Patterns and Proportions in Vergil's Aeneid, a Study in Mathematical Compostion.* Ann Arbor: University of Michigan Press, 1962.

12. Fischer, Oskar. *Orientalische und griechische Zahlensymbolik.* Leipzig: Altmann, 1918 (not seen).

OLD AND MIDDLE HIGH GERMAN LITERATURE

13. Batts, Michael S. "Form as a Criterion in Manuscript Criticism." *MLR* 55 (1960): 543–552.

14. ———. "On the Form of the *Annolied.*" *Monatshefte* 52 (1960): 79–82.

15. ———. *Die Form der Aventiuren im Nibelungenlied.* Giessen: Schmitz, 1961.

16. ———. "Numbers and Number Symbolism in Medieval German Poetry." *MLQ* 24 (1963): 342–349.

17. Betz, Werner. "Zur Zahlensymbolik im Aufbau des *Annoliedes,*" *Mediaeval German Studies presented to Frederick Norman* (London: University of London Institute of Germanic Studies, 1965), pp. 39–45.

18. Eggers, Hans. "Der Liebesmonolog in Eilharts *Tristrant.*" *Euphorion* 45 (1950): 275–304.

19. ———. "Strukturprobleme mittelalterlicher Epik dargestellt am *Parzival* Wolframs von Eschenbach." *Euphorion* 47 (1953): 260–270.

20. ———. *Symmetrie und Proportion epischen Erzählens.* Stuttgart: Klett, 1956.

21. ———. "Vom Formenbau mittelhochdeutscher Epen." *DU* 11 (1959, Heft 2): 81–97.

22. ———. "Der goldene Schnitt im Aufbau alt- und mittelhochdeutscher Epen." *Wirkendes Wort* 10 (1960): 193–203.

23. ———. "Das *Annolied*—eine Exempeldichtung?" *Festschrift für Ludwig Wolff* (Neumünster: Wachholtz, 1962), 161–172.

24. Fourquet, Jean. "Zum Aufbau des *Nibelungenliedes* und des *Kudrunliedes.*" *ZfdA* 85 (1954): 137–149.

25. ———. "La composition du *Pauvre Henri*." *Études germaniques* 16 (1961): 19–23.

26. ———. "Zum Aufbau des *Armen Heinrich*." *Wirkendes Wort*, Sonderheft 3 (1961): 12–24.

27. ———. "Le cryptogramme du *Tristan* et la composition du poème." *Études germaniques* 18 (1963): 271–276.

28. ———. "La composition des livres III à VI du *Parzival*," *Mediaeval German Studies presented to Frederick Norman* (London: University of London Institute of Germanic Studies, 1965), pp. 138–156.

29. Frances, Mary (Mary Frances McCarthy). "Architectonic Symmetry as a Principle of Structure in the *Nibelungenlied*." *Germanic Review* 41 (1966): 157–169. Cf. her "Unity in the Nibelungenlied." Ph.D. dissertation, Johns Hopkins University, 1961.

30. Frings, Theodor, and Schieb, Gabriele. "Heinrich von Veldeke." *Beitr.* 70 (1948): 1–294. Chiefly p. 45 ff. and 179 ff.; see also other studies by the same authors.

31. Fritschi, Karl. *Das Anno-Lied*. Ph.D. dissertation. Zürich. Juris, 1957.

32. Gruenter, Rainer. "Bauformen der Waldlebenepisode in Gotfrids *Tristan und Isolde*," *Gestaltprobleme der Dichtung—Günther Müller zu seinem 65. Geburtstag* (Bonn: Bouvier, 1957), pp. 21–48.

33. Hatto, A. T. "On Beauty of Numbers in Wolfram's Dawn Songs (An Improved Metrical Canon)." *MLR* 45 (1950): 181–188.

34. ———. "Walther von der Vogelweide's Ottonian Poems: A New Interpretation." *Speculum* 24 (1949): 542–553. See the "Appendix: Survey of Strophes."

35. Hempel, Heinrich. "Der Eingang von Wolframs *Parzival*." *ZfdA* 83 (1951/52): 162–180.

36. Henzen, W. "Das 9. Buch des *Parzival*. Überlegungen zum Aufbau," *Erbe der Vergangenheit, Festgabe für Karl Helm* (Tübingen: Niemeyer, 1951), 189–217.

37. Huisman, J. A. *Neue Wege zur dichterischen und musikalischen Technik Walthers von der Vogelweide. Mit einem Exkurs über die symmetrische Zahlenkomposition im Mittelalter*. Utrecht: Kemink en zoon, 1950.

38. Ittenbach, Max. *Deutsche Dichtung der salischen Kaiserzeit und verwandte Denkmäler*. Würzburg: Triltsch, 1937.

39. Janzen, Renate. "Zum Aufbau des *Kudrun*-Epos." *Wirkendes Wort* 12 (1962): 257–273.

40. Kienast, Richard. "Zur Tektonik von Wolframs *Willehalm*," *Studien*

zur deutschen Philologie des Mittelalters, Friedrich Panzer dargebracht (Heidelberg: Winter, 1950), 96–115.

41. Kraus, Carl von. "Das Akrostichon in Gottfrieds *Tristan*." *ZfdA* 50 (1908): 220–222.

42. Kuhn, Hugo. *"Erec," Dichtung und Welt im Mittelalter* (Stuttgart: Metzler, 1959), pp. 133–150 (from *Festschrift für P. Kluckhohn und H. Schneider* [Tübingen: Mohr, 1948], 122–147).

43. ———. "Gestalten und Lebenskräfte der frühmittelhochdeutschen Dichtung," *Dichtung und Welt* . . . , 112–132 (from *DVjs* 27 [1953]: 1–30).

44. Maurer, Friedrich. *Leid; Studien zur Bedeutungs- und Problemgeschichte besonders in den großen Epen der staufischen Zeit.* Bern: Francke, 1951. The chapter on Gottfried's *Tristan* discusses the form.

45. ———. "Über die Formkunst des Dichters unseres *Nibelungenliedes*," *Dichtung und Sprache des Mittelalters* (Bern/Munich: Francke, 1963), 70–79 [from *DU* 6 (1954, Heft 5): 77–83].

46. ———. "Über den Bau der Aventiuren des *Nibelungenliedes*," *Festschrift für Dietrich Kralik* (Horn/N.-Ö.: Berger, 1954), pp. 93–98.

47. ———. "Das alte *Ezzolied*," *Dienendes Wort, eine Festgabe für Ernst Bender* (Karlsruhe; G. Braun, 1959), pp. 1–10.

48. Mergell, Bodo. *Tristan und Isolde; Ursprung und Entwicklung der Tristansage des Mittelalters.* Mainz: Kirchheim, 1949.

49. ———. *"Nibelungenlied* und höfischer Roman." *Euphorion* 45 (1950): 105–136.

50. ———. *"Ezzos Gesang."* Beitr. 76 (1954): 199–216.

51. ———. *"Annolied* und *Kaiserchronik."* Beitr. 77 (Halle, 1955): 124–146.

52. ———. *Der Gral in Wolframs Parzival.* Halle: Niemeyer, 1952.

53. Mohr, Wolfgang. "Vorstudien zum Aufbau von Priester Arnolds *Loblied auf den heiligen Geist (Siebenzahl),"* *Die Wissenschaft von deutscher Sprache und Dichtung, Festschrift für Friedrich Maurer* (Stuttgart: Klett, 1963), pp. 336–351.

54. Morgan, B. Q. "On the Use of Numbers in the *Nibelungenlied."* *JEGP* 36 (1937): 10–20.

55. Ohly, E. F. "Der Prolog des *St. Trudperter Hohen Liedes."* *ZfdA* 84 (1952/53): 198–232.

56. ———. "Wolframs Gebet an den hl. Geist im Eingang des *Willehalm."* *ZfdA* 91 (1961/62): 1–37.

57. Rathofer, Johannes. *Der Heliand. Theologischer Sinn als tektonische Form.* Cologne/Graz: Böhlau, 1962.

58. ———. "Zum Aufbau des *Heliand.*" *ZfdA* 93 (1964): 239–272.

59. ———. "Zum Bauplan von Otfrids *Evangelienbuch.*" *ZfdA* 94 (1965): 36–38.

60. Roeland, J. G. "Bilaterale Symmetrie bei Gottfried von Straßburg." *Neophil.* 27 (1942): 281–290.

61. Rupp, Heinz. *Deutsche religiöse Dichtungen des 11. und 12. Jahrhunderts.* Freiburg/Br.: Herder, 1958.

62. ———. "Rudolf von Ems' *Barlaam und Josaphat,*" *Dienendes Wort, eine Festgabe für Ernst Bender* (Karlsruhe: G. Braun, 1959), pp. 11–37.

63. ———. "Über den Bau epischer Dichtungen des Mittelalters," *Die Wissenschaft . . .,* pp. 366–382.

64. ———. "Otfrid von Weissenburg und die Zahlen." *Archiv* 201 (1964): 262–265.

65. Schirmer, Karl-Heinz. *Die Strophik Walthers von der Vogelweide. Ein Beitrag zu den Aufbauprinzipien in der lyrischen Dichtung des Hochmittelalters.* Halle: VEB Niemeyer, 1956.

66. ———. "Zum Aufbau des hochmittelalterlichen deutschen Strophenliedes." *DU* 11 (1959, Heft 2): 35–59.

67. Scholte, J. H. "Symmetrie in Gottfrieds *Tristan,*" *Vom Werden des deutschen Geistes. Festgabe Gustav Ehrismann* (Berlin: de Gruyter, 1925), pp. 66–79.

68. ———. "Gottfrieds *Tristan*-Einleitung." *ZfdPh* 57 (1932): 25–32.

69. ———. "Gottfrieds von Straßburg Initialenspiel." *Beitr.* 65 (1942): 280–302.

70. Schröder, W. J. "Der dichterische Plan des *Parzival*romans." *Beitr.* 74 (Halle, 1952): 160–192.

71. Schupp, Volker. "Die *Auslegung des Vaterunsers* und ihre Bauform." *DU* 11 (1959, Heft 2): 25–34.

72. ———. *Septenar und Bauform. Studien zur Auslegung des Vaterunsers, zu De VII Sigillis und zum Palästinalied Walthers von der Vogelweide.* Berlin: Erich Schmidt, 1964.

73. Sünger, Maria Therese. *Studien zur Struktur der Wiener und Milstätter Genesis.* Klagenfurt: Geschichtsverein für Kärnten, 1964.

74. Swinburne, Hilda. "Numbers in Otfrids *Evangelienbuch.*" *MLR* 52 (1957): 195–202.

75. Tax, Petrus W. *Wort, Sinnbild, Zahl im Tristanroman.* Berlin: Erich Schmidt, 1961.

76. ——. "Studien zum Symbolischen in Hartmanns *Erec*: Enites Pferd." *ZfdPh* 82 (1963): 29–44.

77. ——. "Studien zum Symbolischen in Hartmanns *Erec*: Erecs ritterliche Erhöhung." *Wirkendes Wort* 13 (1963): 277–288.

78. ——. "Bilaterale Symmetrie bei Otfrid." *MLN* 80 (1965): 490–491.

79. Taylor, R. J. "A Song by Prince Wizlav of Rügen." *MLR* 46 (1951): 31–37.

80. Thomas, H. "Der altdeutsche Strophenbau und die unliturgische Sequenz," *Festgruß für Hans Pyritz* (Sonderheft des Euphorion, Heidelberg: Winter, 1955), pp. 14–20.

81. Tschirch, Fritz. "Schlüsselzahlen. Studie zur geistigen Durchdringung der Form in der deutschen Dichtung des Mittelalters," *Beiträge zur deutschen und nordischen Literatur, Festgabe für Leopold Magon* (Berlin: Akademie, 1958), pp. 30–53. Discussion also of acrosticha.

82. ——. "Wernhers *Helmbrecht* in der Nachfolge von Gottfrieds *Tristan.*" *Beitr.* 80 (Tübingen, 1958): 292–314.

83. ——. "Zum symbolbestimmten Umfang mittelalterlicher Dichtungen," *Stil- und Formprobleme in der Literatur* (*Vorträge beim 7. Kongress der Int. Vereinigung f.mod.Sp.u.Lit.in Heidelberg* [Heidelberg: Winter, 1959]), pp. 148–156.

84. ——. "Die Bedeutung der Rundzahl 100 für den Umfang mittelalterlicher Dichtungen," *Gestalt und Glaube, Festschrift für Oskar Söhngen* (Berlin: Merseburger; Witten: Luther-Verlag, 1960), pp. 78–88, 236 f. Chiefly concerned with the use of the Ave Maria of 100 letters in acrostica and so on.

85. ——. "17 - 34 - 153. Der heilsgeschichtliche Symbolgrund im *Gregorius* Hartmanns von Aue," *Formenwandel. Festschrift zum 65. Geburtstag von Paul Böckmann* (Hamburg: Hoffmann und Campe, 1964), pp. 27–46.

86. Wiehl, Peter. "Über den Aufbau des *Nibelungenliedes.*" *Wirkendes Wort* 16 (1966): 309–323.

87. Wiget, Wilhelm. "Zu den Widmungen Otfrids." *Beitr.* 49 (1925): 441–444.

88. Willems, Fritz. "Der parataktische Satzstil im *Ludwigslied.*" *ZfdA* 85 (1954): 18–35.

ADDENDUM: M. Huby. "La Structure Numérique et sa Valeur Symbolique dans la Poésie Religieuse Allemande du Moyen Âge. *EG* (1967) (Discussion of items 72 and 73).

NOTE: 81, 83, 84, and 85 now revised in Fritz Tschirch, *Spiegelungen* (Berlin: Eric Schmidt Verlag, 1966), Ch. III, "Figurale Komposition in mittelalterlicher deutscher Dictung."

ANALYTICAL INDEX TO THE BIBLIOGRAPHY

NOTES ON CONTRIBUTORS

RONALD J. TAYLOR is professor of German in the School of European Studies at The University of Sussex. He has edited works in both English and German, including *E. T. A. Hoffmann, Das Fräulein von Scuderi* (1966). His book (with A. T. Hatto), *The Songs of Neidhart von Reuental* (1958), is an excellent treatment of the metrics and musicology of that poet. His *Melodien der weltlichen Lieder des Mittelalters* (1964) has become a standard reference work in *Minnesang* musicology, while his two-volume work *The Art of the Minnesinger* (1968) contains all known melodies by Minnesingers of the 12th and 13th centuries. In the modern field he has published a study of E. T. A. Hoffmann (1964) and a number of translations of German Romantic authors.

HUGO KUHN is a renowned scholar of medieval German literature. He was professor of German philology at Tübingen and is now at Munich. He has served as editor of *Deutsche Vierteljahrsschrift* since 1949. His major books include *Minnesangs Wende* (1952), *Die Klassik des Rittertums* (1952), and a collection of his essays: *Dichtung und Welt im Mittelalter* (1959). Professor Kuhn is known especially also for his association with the monumental edition of the thirteenth century German lyrics by Carl von Kraus, *Deutsche Liederdichter des 13. Jahrhunderts* (2 vols., 1952 and 1958), and for the shorter edition derived from this, *Minnesang des 13. Jahrhunderts* (1962).

WILLIAM T. H. JACKSON, who is currently Chairman of the Department of German at Columbia University, is a specialist in medieval literature and thought. Among his important books in this field are

The Literature of the Middle Ages (1960), *Essential Works of Erasmus* (1965), *An Anthology of German Literature 800–1750* (with Peter Demetz, 1968), and *Medieval Lyrics in Translation* (1967). He has been both a Guggenheim Fellow and a Phi Beta Kappa Visiting Scholar; he was Editor of *The Germanic Review* from 1954–1965.

HUBERT HEINEN is Associate Professor of German at the University of Pittsburgh and a rare devotee of metrical theory and practice. His book on the metrics of Hans Folz *Die rhythmisch-metrische Gestaltung des Knittelverses bei Hans Folz* (1966) is a major contribution to the rethinking of this thorny question.

MICHAEL S. BATTS is Professor and Head of the Department of German at The University of British Columbia (Vancouver). He has among his many publications several on the question of numbers in literature, the subject of his present essay. These are listed in the welcome bibliography he has contributed to this volume. His books include *Die Form der Aventiuren im Nibelungenlied* (1961), *Bruder Hansens Marienlieder* (1963), and *Studien zu Bruder Hansens Marienliedern* (1964).

frequentatio: 64
Frey, Dagobert: on art as successive unfolding of a form, 30
Friedrich von Hausen: 37

Gaiser, Gerd: his numerically structured novels, 96 n
Gedrut: his view of high *Minnesang,* 35
Geltar: his view of high *Minnesang,* 35
Gennrich, Friedrich: his notation of Neidhart's *Sommerlied,* 88–90
Georgics: examined for numerical composition, 100–101, 107
Gottfried von Neifen: cadences of, 86–87
Gottfried von Strassburg: for description of performance of epic lays, 19; his use of terms indicating polyphony, 20
Gregorian chant: as source of melodic vocabulary of secular singers, 14; as one source of medieval monodies, 22–23; not suitable as source of rhythmical patterns, 82 n

Hagen, Friedrich Heinrich von der: as earliest editor to provide musical notations of *Minnesang,* 9
Hartmann von Aue: his description of musical performance, 19; his crusade song, 31–41
Hatto, A. T.: criticized by Schirmer, 106; uses structural patterns in establishing chronology, 111
Haupt, Moriz: as early critical editor, 9
Hebungsspaltung: notation of, 88 n
Heinrich von Melk: his satire on boastful knights, 35
Heinrich von Morungen: his original

melodies not extant, 13; his song with *ich var* theme, 32
Heliand: use of 3 and 4 significant in, 107
Heusler, Andreas: rejects earlier attempts to link metrics and musicology, 81; on isochronic rhythm in German verse, 82
Hieatt, A. K.: on numbers in Spenser's *Epithalamion,* 98, 101
Hincmar, Bishop: makes only medieval reference to workshop practice, 103
hohe Minne: 37–39
Huismann, J. A.: on the *Marienleich,* 105; on the *Ludwigslied,* 109

ich var theme: 32–33
Isaac, Heinrich: as composer of "Innsbruck ich muss dich lassen . . .," 36 n
Ittenbach, Max: his early study of numerical composition, 97; his analysis of *Ludwigslied,* 109

Jenaer Liederhandschrift: as only major manuscript with musical notations, 12
Johannes de Garlandia: as medieval musical theorist, 24 n
1 John 4:19: as source of theme of "God who first loved us," 35
Jungbluth, Günther: his conjecture for removing the crux in Hartmann's crusade song, 38
Jüngerer Titurel: its music as a link between epic and lyrical genres, 19–20

"Kalenda maya": 25
Kienast, Richard: his analysis of Wolfram's *Willehalm,* 100